W9-BVL-823

Alfred's max™

see it ◉ hear it ◉ play it

Learn to play
Guitar
Complete

RON MANUS

L. C. HARNSBERGER

Alfred's MAX™ is the next best thing to having your own private teacher. No confusion, no frustration, no guesswork—just lessons that are well paced and easy to follow. You listen to the music you're learning to play and watch a professional show how it's done, then get time to stretch out and put it all together. No matter how you like to learn, Alfred's MAX™ series gives you the ultimate learning experience at a screamin' deal of a price.

Cover photos: Martin D-28 guitar courtesy of Martin Guitar Company. Electric guitar courtesy of Daisy Rock Guitars, photograph by Karen Miller.

Alfred

Book and DVD (with case)
ISBN-10: 0-7390-4170-3
ISBN-13: 978-0-7390-4170-3

Book and DVD (without case)
ISBN-10: 0-7390-4208-4
ISBN-13: 978-0-7390-4208-3

2

CONTENTS

Level 1

Level 2

About the DVD

The DVD contains valuable demonstrations of all the instructional material in the book. You will get the best results by following along with your book as you watch these video segments. Musical examples that are not performed with video are included as audio tracks on the DVD for listening and playing along.

THE PARTS OF THE GUITAR

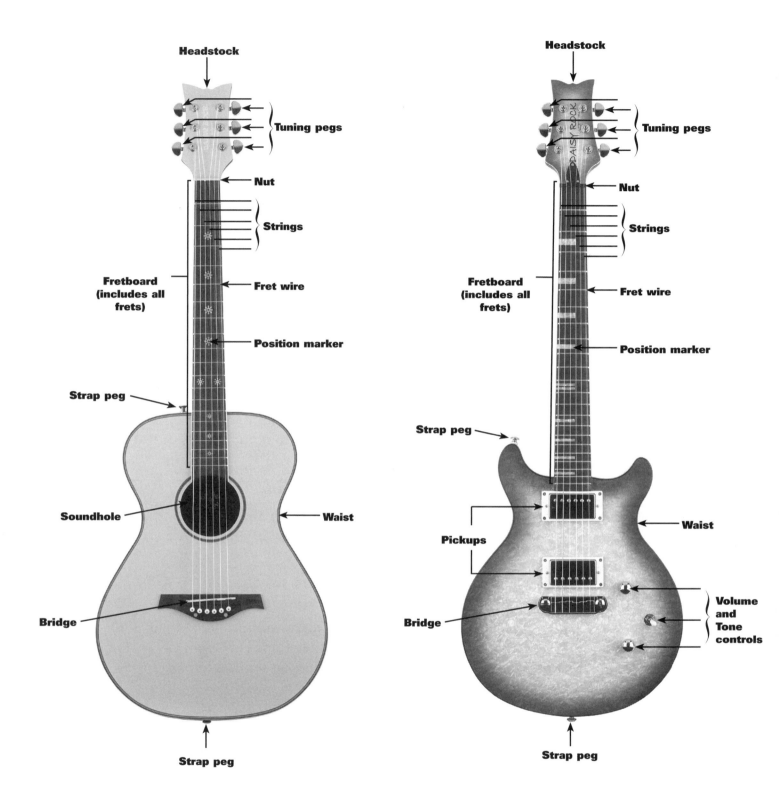

Headstock

Tuning pegs

Nut

Strings

Fretboard (includes all frets)

Fret wire

Position marker

Strap peg

Soundhole

Bridge

Waist

Strap peg

Headstock

Tuning pegs

Nut

Strings

Fretboard (includes all frets)

Fret wire

Position marker

Strap peg

Pickups

Bridge

Waist

Volume and Tone controls

Strap peg

Steel Strings and Nylon Strings
Steel strings are found on both acoustic and electric guitars.
They have a bright and brassy sound.

Nylon strings are usually found on classical and flamenco guitars.
They have a mellow, delicate sound. Nylon strings are often easier for
beginners to play because they are easier on the fingers than steel strings.

HOW TO HOLD YOUR GUITAR

Below are three ways to hold your guitar.
Pick the one that is most comfortable for you.

When playing, keep your left wrist away from the fingerboard. This will allow your fingers to be in a better position to finger the chords. Press your fingers firmly, but make certain they do not touch the neighboring strings.

Sitting.

Sitting with legs crossed.

Standing with strap.

THE RIGHT HAND

To *strum* means to play the strings with your right hand by brushing quickly across them. There are two common ways of strumming the strings. One is with a pick, and the other is with your fingers.

Strumming with a Pick
Hold the pick between your thumb and index finger. Hold it firmly, but don't squeeze it too hard.

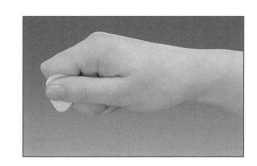

Strum from the sixth string (the thickest, lowest-sounding string) to the first string (the thinnest, highest-sounding string).

Start near the top string.

Move mostly your wrist, not just your arm. Finish near the bottom string.

Important:
Strum by mostly moving your wrist, not just your arm. Use as little motion as possible. Start as close to the top string as you can, and never let your hand move past the edge of the guitar.

Strumming with Your Fingers
First, decide if you feel more comfortable strumming with the side of your thumb or the nail of your index finger. The strumming motion is the same with the thumb or finger as it is when using the pick. Strum from the sixth string (the thickest, lowest-sounding string) to the first string (the thinnest, highest-sounding string).

Strumming with the thumb.

Strumming with the index finger.

Here is a great exercise to get used to strumming.

Let's Strum
Strum all six strings slowly and evenly. Count your strums out loud as you play.
Repeat this exercise until you feel comfortable strumming the strings.

	strum	strum	strum	strum	strum	strum	strum	strum
	/	/	/	/	/	/	/	/
Count:	1	2	3	4	5	6	7	8

THE LEFT HAND

Proper Left-Hand Position

Learning to use your left-hand fingers starts with a
good hand position. Place your hand so your thumb
rests comfortably in the middle of the back of the neck.
Position your fingers on the front of the neck as if you
are gently squeezing a ball between them and your thumb.
Keep your elbow in and your fingers curved.

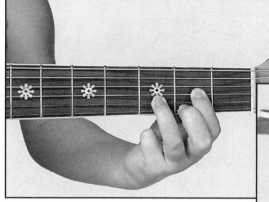

Keep elbow in and fingers curved.

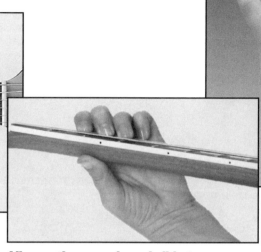

Like gently squeezing a ball between your
fingertips and thumb.

Placing a Finger on a String

When you press a string
with a left-hand finger,
make sure you press firmly
with the tip of your finger
and as close to the fret wire
as you can without actually
being right on it. Short
fingernails are important!
This will create a clean,
bright tone.

RIGHT
Finger presses the string
down near the fret with-
out actually being on it.

WRONG
Finger is too far from fret
wire; tone is "buzzy"
and indefinite.

WRONG
Finger is on top of fret
wire; tone is muffled and
unclear.

How to Read Chord Diagrams

Fingering diagrams show where to place the fingers of your left
hand. Strings that are not played are shown with a dashed line.
The finger that is to be pressed down is shown as a circle with a
number in it. The number indicates which finger is used. The
diagram at the right shows the first finger on the first fret.

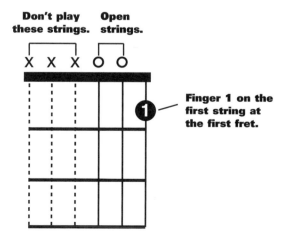

Don't play
these strings.

Open
strings.

Finger 1 on the
first string at
the first fret.

TUNING YOUR GUITAR

First, make sure your strings are wound properly around the tuning pegs. They should go from the inside to the outside as illustrated to the right. Some guitars have all six tuning pegs on the same side of the headstock. If this is the case, make sure all six strings are wound the same way, from the inside out.

Turning a tuning peg clockwise makes the pitch lower. Turning a tuning peg counterclockwise makes the pitch higher. Be sure not to tune the strings too high because they could break.

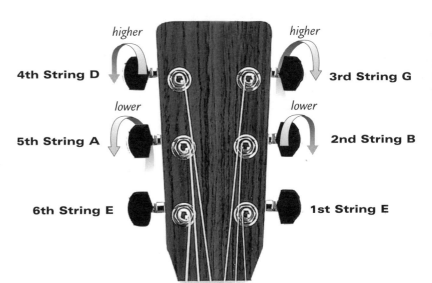

Important:

Always remember that the thinnest, highest-sounding string, the one closest to the floor, is the first string. The thickest, lowest-sounding string, the one closest to the ceiling, is the sixth string. When guitarists say "the highest string," they are referring to the highest-sounding string.

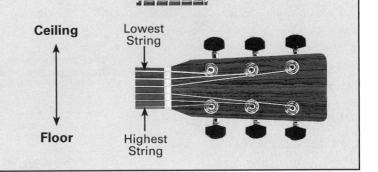

Using the DVD
When tuning while watching the DVD, listen to the directions and match each of your guitar's strings to the corresponding pitches on the DVD.

Tuning the Guitar to Itself
When your sixth string is in tune, you can tune the rest of the strings using the guitar alone. First, tune the sixth string to E on the piano:

Then, follow the instructions below to get the guitar in tune.

Press 5th fret of 6th string to get pitch of 5th string (A).

Press 5th fret of 5th string to get pitch of 4th string (D).

Press 5th fret of 4th string to get pitch of 3rd string (G).

Press 4th fret of 3rd string to get pitch of 2nd string (B).

Press 5th fret of 2nd string to get pitch of 1st string (E).

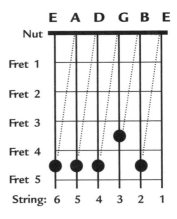

Pitch Pipes and Electronic Tuners
If you don't have a piano available, consider buying an electronic tuner or pitch pipe. There are many types available, and a salesperson at your local music store can help you decide which is best for you.

THE BASICS OF READING MUSIC

Musical sounds are indicated by symbols called *notes.*
Their time value is determined by their color (white or black)
and by stems or flags attached to the note.

The Staff

The notes are named after the first seven letters of the alphabet (A–G), which are repeated to embrace the entire range of musical sound. The name and pitch of a note are determined by the note's position on five horizontal lines and four spaces between called the *staff.*

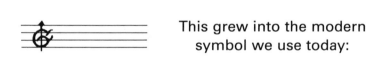

The Treble Clef

During the evolution of musical notation, the staff had from 2 to 20 lines, and symbols were invented to locate certain lines and the pitch of the note on that line. These symbols were called *clefs.*

Music for the guitar is written in the *G clef* or *treble clef.* Originally the Gothic letter G was used on a four-line staff to establish the pitch of G.

This grew into the modern symbol we use today:

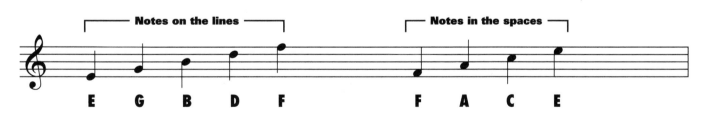

Measures (Bars)

Music is also divided into equal parts called *measures* or *bars.* One measure is divided from another by a *bar line:*

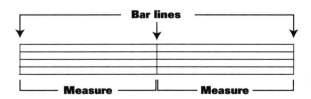

NOTES ON THE FIRST STRING E

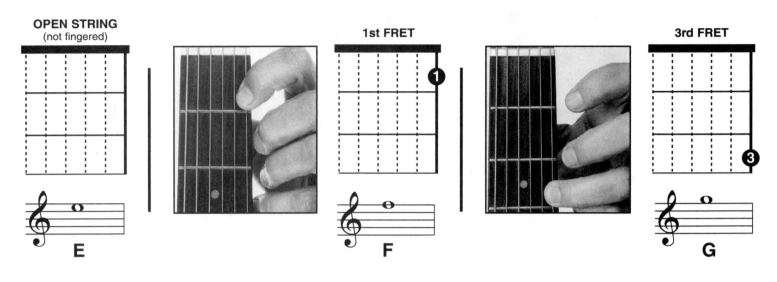

OPEN STRING (not fingered)

E

1st FRET

F

3rd FRET

G

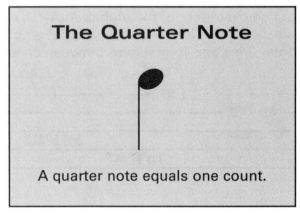

The Quarter Note

A quarter note equals one count.

Play this example slowly and evenly. Use down-strokes for all the music in this book.

Go to the next line without stopping.

A *double bar* line indicates the end of a piece.

Playing E, F and G on My Extra Fine Guitar

Once Again

When you play the F on the 1st fret and follow it with the G on the 3rd fret, keep the first finger down.
You will only hear the G, but when you go back to the F, it will sound smooth.

HOLD F DOWN - - - - - - -¬

Extra Credit

Make sure to place your left-hand fingers as close to the fret wires as possible without touching them.

HOLD F DOWN - - - - - - -¬   HOLD F DOWN - -

COUNTING TIME

Four Kinds of Notes

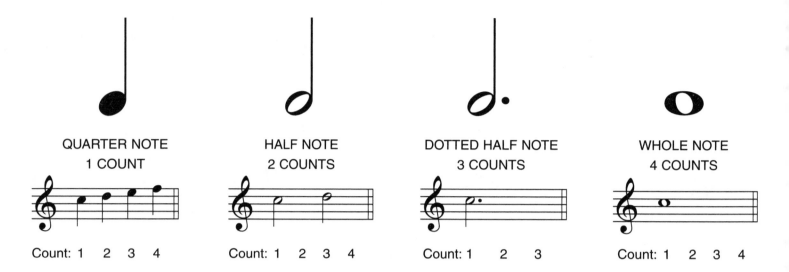

| QUARTER NOTE | HALF NOTE | DOTTED HALF NOTE | WHOLE NOTE |
| 1 COUNT | 2 COUNTS | 3 COUNTS | 4 COUNTS |

Count: 1 2 3 4   Count: 1 2 3 4   Count: 1 2 3   Count: 1 2 3 4

Time Signatures

Each piece of music has numbers at the beginning called a *time signature*.
These numbers tell us how to count time.

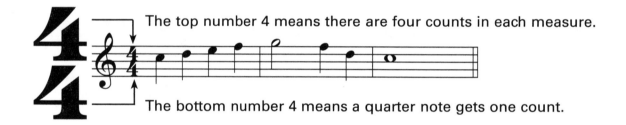

The top number 4 means there are four counts in each measure.

The bottom number 4 means a quarter note gets one count.

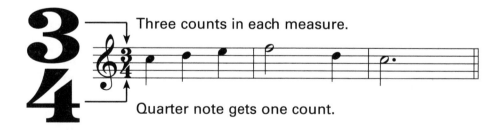

Three counts in each measure.

Quarter note gets one count.

IMPORTANT: Fill in the missing time signatures of the songs already learned.

NOTES ON THE SECOND STRING B

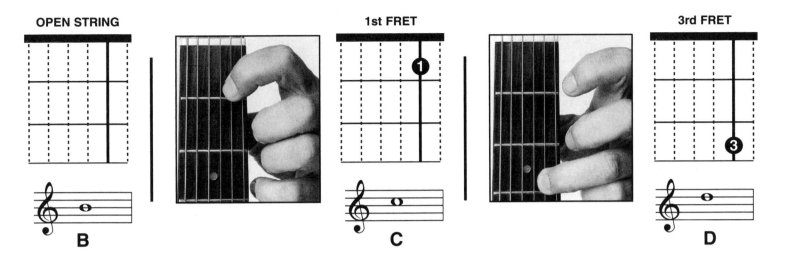

OPEN STRING B

1st FRET C

3rd FRET D

Count: 1 2 3 4   1 2 3 4   (etc.)

Jammin' on Two Strings

Count: 1 2 3 4   (etc.)

Up Two Flights

Count: 1   2   3   1   2   3   (etc.)

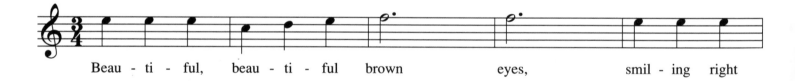

Beautiful Brown Eyes

Beau - ti - ful,   beau - ti - ful   brown   eyes,   smil - ing   right

in - to   my   heart.   But   now   where   are   those   beau - ti - ful

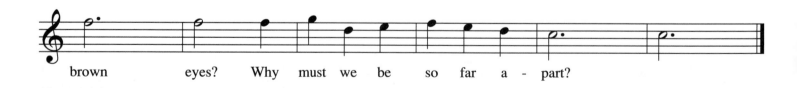

brown   eyes?   Why   must   we   be   so   far   a - part?

Rockin' Guitar

Letters called *chord symbols* that are placed above each staff may be used for a duet.
Either have a friend or teacher play the chords while you play the notes, or play along with the
audio tracks on the DVD. Many of the tunes in the rest of this book include chords for duets.

Eric Johnson is widely accepted as one of the
most influential and gifted guitarists of the
twentieth century. Born in Austin, Texas, he
was only 16 when his immense talent was
recognized, and by 21 he'd begun playing in
legendary bands that came to include the
Electromagnets, the Eric Johnson Group, and
Avenue. After naming him Best Overall Guitarist
for four consecutive years, *Guitar Player*
magazine inducted him into their Gallery of
Greats in 1995.

Jingle Bells

Jin - gle bells! Jin - gle bells! Jin - gle all the

way! Oh, what fun it is to ride a

one - horse o - pen sleigh! Jin - gle bells!

Jin - gle bells! Jin - gle all the way!

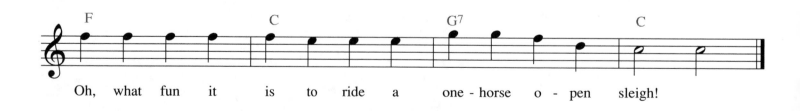

Oh, what fun it is to ride a one - horse o - pen sleigh!

NOTES ON THE THIRD STRING G

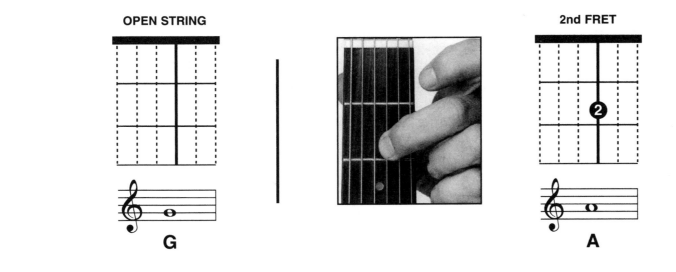

OPEN STRING

G

2nd FRET

A

Jammin' on Three Strings

DUET: G7

C

G7

D   C   G

Au Clair de la Lune

Largo

from the New World Symphony

Dvořák

REPEAT SIGNS

"Aura Lee" is an old American folk song that was later recorded by Elvis Presley and called "Love Me Tender." This music uses *repeat signs.* The double dots inside the double bars tell you that everything between those double bars is to be repeated.

Aura Lee

Dubbed the "King of Rock and Roll," Elvis Presley influenced several generations of young people to play guitar and may have had more impact on contemporary culture than any other figure in music.

CHORDS

A *chord* is a combination of three or more notes played at the same time.
All the notes are connected by a stem unless they are whole notes, which have no stem.
The stems can go either up or down.

Two-Note Exercise

This exercise will get you used to playing two notes at a time—open B and open E.
Play both strings together with one down-stroke.

Three-Note Chord Exercise

This is the first time you are playing three-note chords.
All the chords in this exercise are made up of the open G, B and E strings.
Play it with your wrist free and relaxed. Remember to keep your eyes on the notes and not your hands.

THREE-STRING C CHORD

 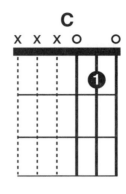

The Quarter Rest

It tells you to be silent for one count.

To make the rest very clear, stop the sound of the strings by touching the strings lightly with the heel of your right hand.

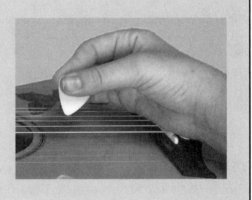

Ode to Joy
Theme from Beethoven's Ninth Symphony

Beethoven

THREE-STRING G⁷ CHORD

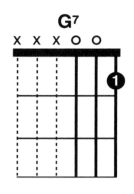

Jammin' with Two Chords

First, play the written notes and learn the melody, then play just the chords and sing.
The slanted lines following a chord symbol mean to play that same chord for each slash.
You repeat the same chord until a new chord symbol appears.

Love Somebody

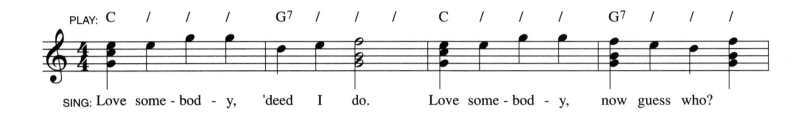

SING: Love some - bod - y, 'deed I do. Love some - bod - y, now guess who?

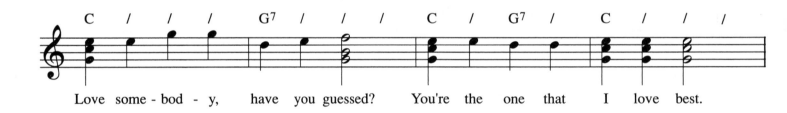

Love some - bod - y, have you guessed? You're the one that I love best.

Love some - bod - y, want to hear? Let me whis - per in your ear.

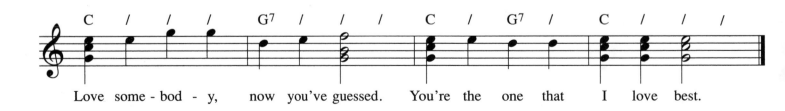

Love some - bod - y, now you've guessed. You're the one that I love best.

THREE-STRING G CHORD

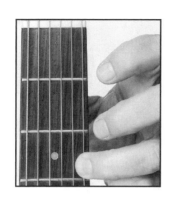

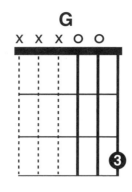

She'll Be Comin' 'Round the Mountain

First, play the written notes and learn the melody, then play just the chords and sing.

Down in the Valley

PLAY: C / / / / / / / / / / / G / / / / /

SING: Down in the val - ley, val - ley so low,

G / / G⁷ / / / / / / / / C / / / / /

Hang your head o - ver, hear the wind blow.

C / / / / / / / / / / / G / / / / /

Ros - es love sun - shine, vio - lets love dew.

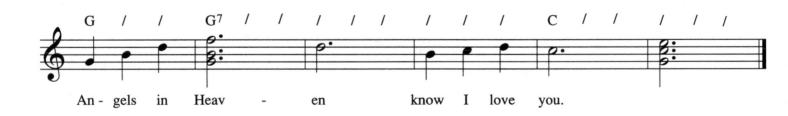

G / / G⁷ / / / / / / / / C / / / / /

An - gels in Heav - en know I love you.

NOTES ON THE FOURTH STRING D

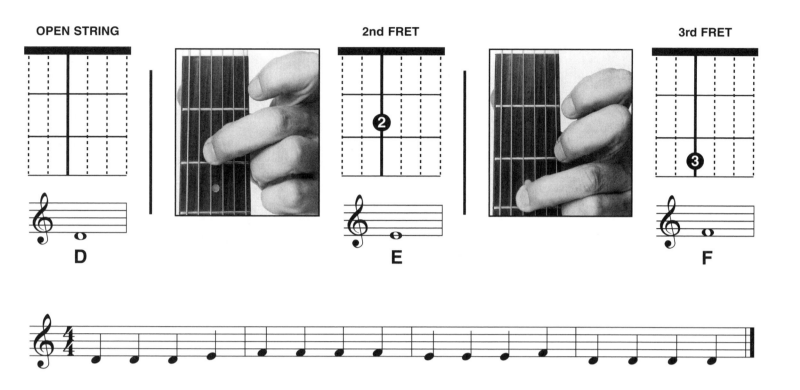

Old MacDonald Had a Farm

"Reuben Reuben" uses a *fermata* (𝄐), which is also called a *hold sign* or *pause sign*. This sign tells you to lengthen the value of the note (usually twice its normal value).

Reuben Reuben

C Blues

𝄴 stands for *common time,* which is the same as $\frac{4}{4}$ time.

Photo: Cesar Vera, courtesy MCA

Blues legend B. B. King has been making his guitar, "Lucille," sing for many years, moving generations of fans with his soulful, heartfelt music. Since the launch of his professional career in the 1950s, his desire to improve the status and acceptability of the blues has set him apart from other players, and he is now commonly referred to as the "greatest living blues guitarist."

Merry Widow Waltz

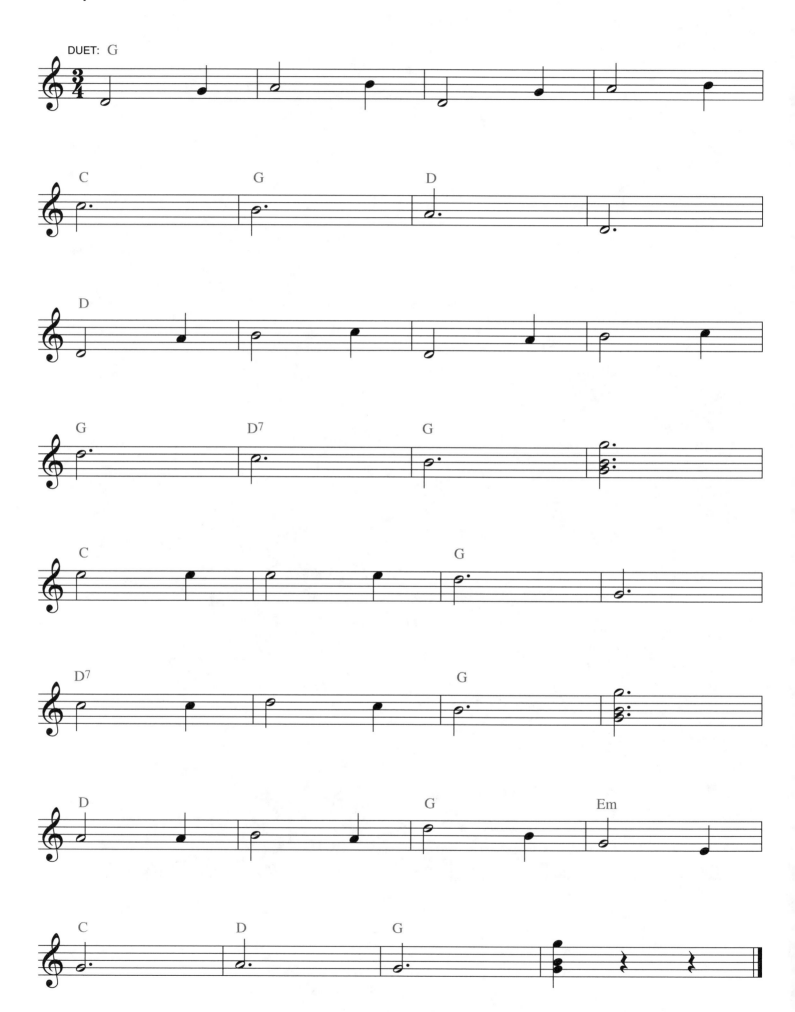

Now that you are getting better at playing chords, here is a song that will be lots of fun to play.
In "Daisy Bell," you will be going from one note, to two notes, to three notes.

Daisy Bell

FOUR-STRING G & G⁷ CHORDS

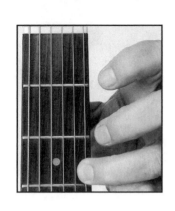

G
x x o o o

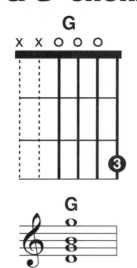

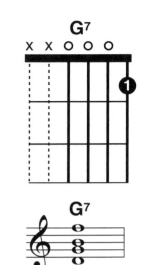

G⁷
x x o o o

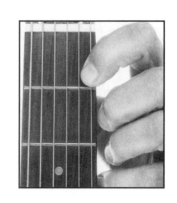

Although these new chords have the same names as chords you have already learned, they use four notes and sound more full.

Rock Me Mozart!

Mozart

With a penchant for outrageous stage antics like lighting his guitar on fire, Jimi Hendrix was one of the most influential guitarists of his generation. Though he lived only a short life, his place in history as one of rock's greatest legends is solidified by his amazing technique and brilliant songwriting.

Photo: Courtesy of Reprise Records.

NOTES ON THE FIFTH STRING A

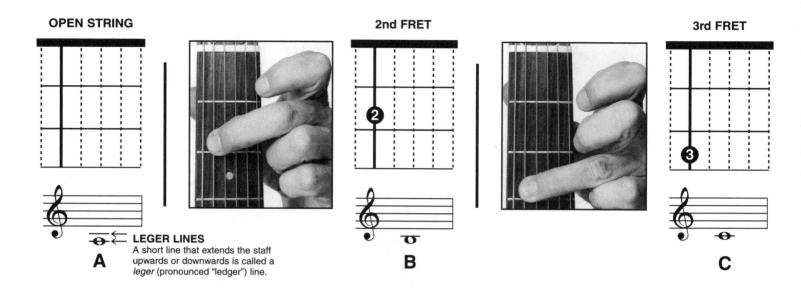

OPEN STRING

LEGER LINES
A short line that extends the staff upwards or downwards is called a *leger* (pronounced "ledger") line.

A

2nd FRET

B

3rd FRET

C

Volga Boatmen

DUET: Am — Dm — Am — Dm — Am

F — C — G — Am — Dm — Am

Peter Gray

A Minor Boogie

"Liebesträum" was written in 1845 by the famous composer Franz Liszt. The title means "love dream."

Liebesträum

Liszt

HIGH A

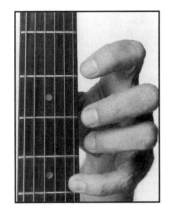  

5th FRET

A

Back in Russia

First, play the written notes and learn the melody, then play just the chords and sing.

The Riddle Song

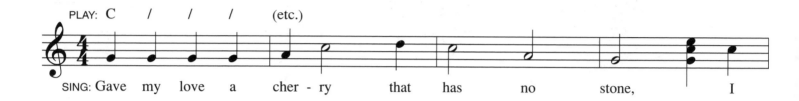

PLAY: C / / / (etc.)

SING: Gave my love a cher - ry that has no stone, I

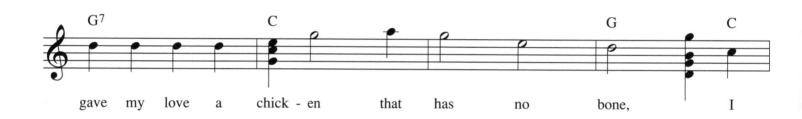

gave my love a chick - en that has no bone, I

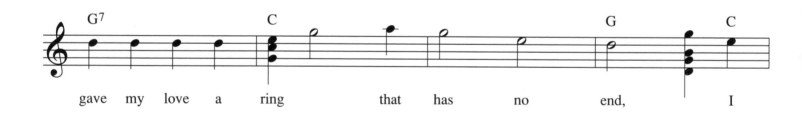

gave my love a ring that has no end, I

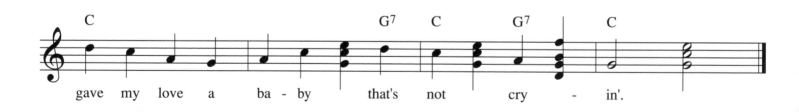

gave my love a ba - by that's not cry - in'.

INCOMPLETE MEASURES

Not all pieces of music begin on the first beat.
Sometimes, music begins with an incomplete measure called a *pickup*.

If the pickup is one beat, the last measure will only have three beats in $\frac{4}{4}$, or two beats in $\frac{3}{4}$.

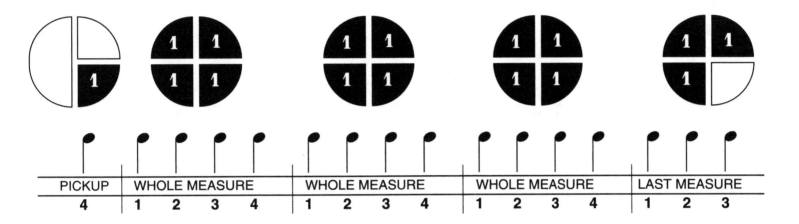

PICKUP	WHOLE MEASURE	WHOLE MEASURE	WHOLE MEASURE	LAST MEASURE
4	1 2 3 4	1 2 3 4	1 2 3 4	1 2 3

A-Tisket, A-Tasket

DUET: C

COUNT: 4

The Yellow Rose of Texas

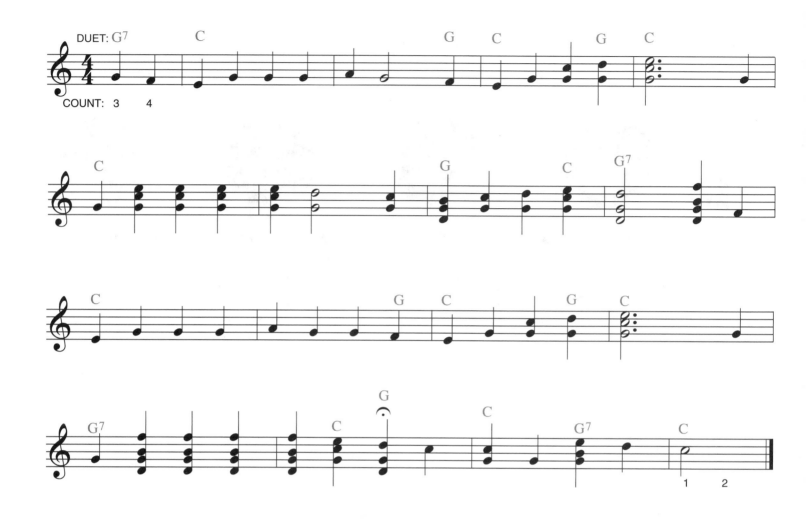

Texas guitarist Stevie Ray Vaughan brought the blues to an entire generation of music lovers and was admired by the likes of Eric Clapton, David Bowie and Buddy Guy for his extraordinary skill. Tragically, a plane crash claimed the life of this celebrated guitar legend in 1990.

NOTES ON THE SIXTH STRING E

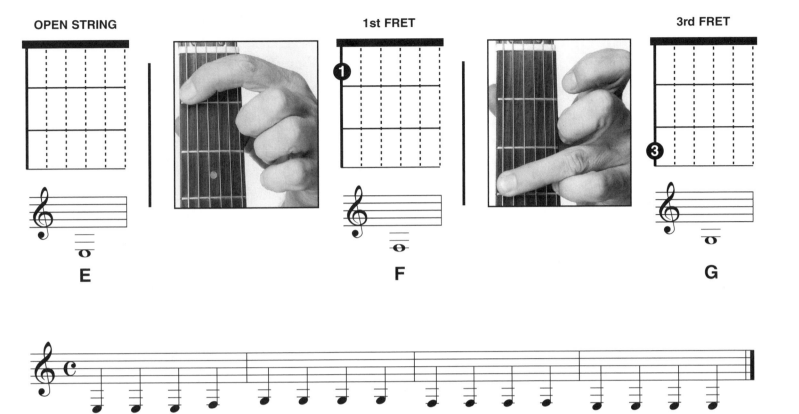

| OPEN STRING | | 1st FRET | | 3rd FRET |

E   F   G

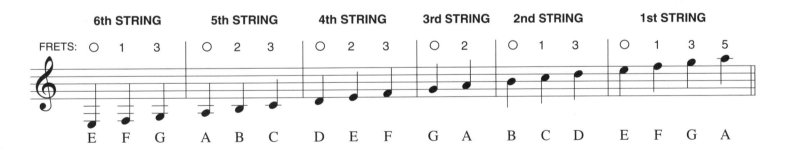

All the Notes You've Learned So Far

| 6th STRING | 5th STRING | 4th STRING | 3rd STRING | 2nd STRING | 1st STRING |

FRETS: O 1 3   O 2 3   O 2 3   O 2   O 1 3   O 1 3 5

E F G   A B C   D E F   G A   B C D   E F G A

TEMPO SIGNS

A *tempo* sign tells you how fast to play music. The three most common tempo signs are below:

Andante (SLOW)   **Moderato** (MODERATELY)   **Allegro** (FAST)

Three-Tempo Rock

Play three times: 1st time **Andante**, 2nd time **Moderato**, 3rd time **Allegro**.

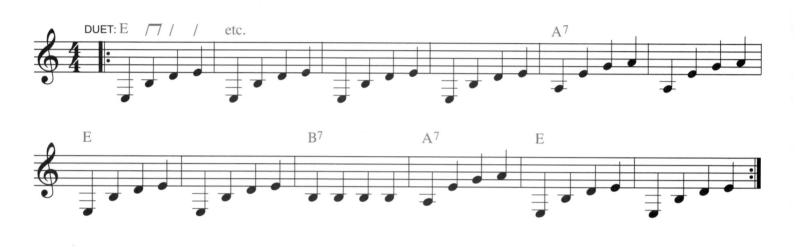

1812 Overture

Theme from Carmen

Bizet

BASS-CHORD ACCOMPANIMENT

A great way to accompany songs is to break up chords by playing a single note followed by a smaller chord. You can take all the chords you have learned so far and create *bass-chord accompaniments.*

The easiest way is to play only the lowest note (called the *bass note*) on the 1st beat and then the rest of the chord on the 2nd, 3rd and 4th beats. That complete pattern is called **bass-chord-chord-chord.** A variation of this pattern repeats the bass note again on the 3rd beat for a **bass-chord-bass-chord** pattern. Here is an example that uses both patterns.

In "Can-Can," both a melody part and accompaniment part are written out.
You can play with a friend, teacher or the DVD. Be sure to learn both parts.

Can-Can (duet)

Offenbach

Note: Part 2 is written in bass-chord-chord-chord style.
It can also be played in bass-chord-bass-chord style.

HOLD E DOWN _____

HOLD E DOWN _____

HOLD C _____

Since the early 1960s, songwriter and performer Bob Dylan has inspired countless fans of both folk music and rock 'n' roll with equal success.

DYNAMICS

Symbols that show how soft or loud to play are called *dynamics*. These symbols come from Italian words. The four most common dynamics are shown here:

Theme from Beethoven's Fifth Symphony

HALF RESTS & WHOLE RESTS

We already learned about a quarter rest equaling one beat.
Here are two more rests:

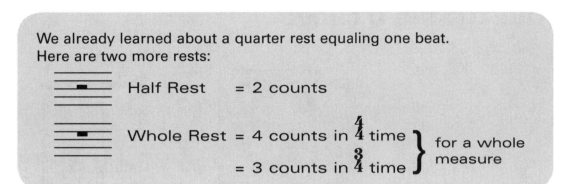

Half Rest = 2 counts

Whole Rest = 4 counts in $\frac{4}{4}$ time ⎫ for a whole
          = 3 counts in $\frac{3}{4}$ time ⎭ measure

The Desert Song

Moderato

FOUR-STRING C CHORD

  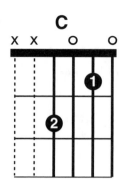

This chord is the first one that uses two fingers at the same time. Finger the three-string C chord, and also place your second finger on the 2nd fret of the 4th string.

Echo Rock

TIES

A *tie* is a curved line that joins two or more notes of the same pitch. When two notes are tied, the second is not played separately, but its value is instead added to the first note.

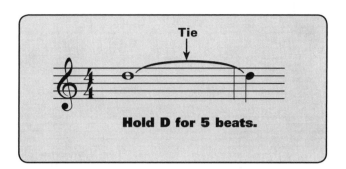

Shenandoah

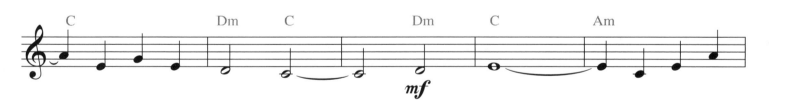

When the Saints Go Marching In (duet or trio*)

Moderato

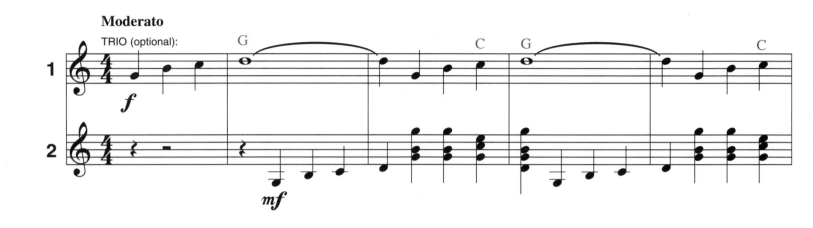

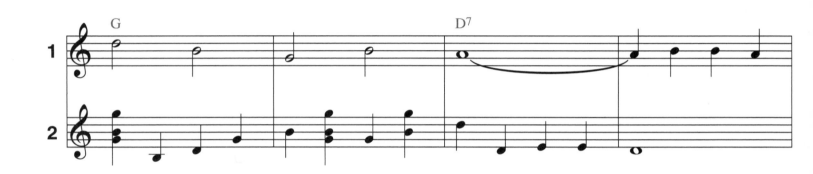

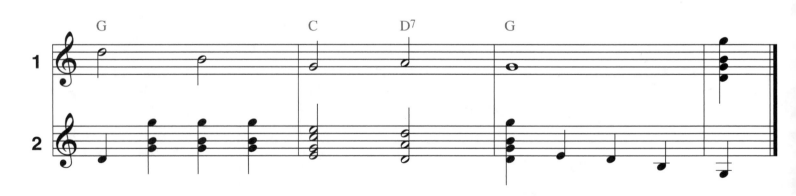

*A *trio* is performed by three players.

MORE BASS-CHORD ACCOMPANIMENTS

When you're in $\frac{3}{4}$ time, the bass-chord-chord accompaniment works great. The bass note is the lowest note in the chord and often the note that gives the chord its name (C for the C chord, G for the G or G⁷ chords, etc.). First, play the bass note alone, then play the rest of the chord on the second and third beats.

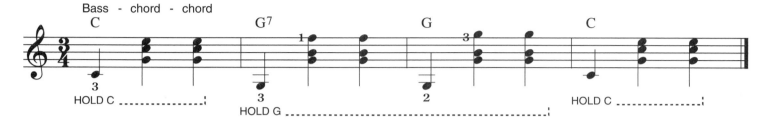

To change things around a bit, you can use another note
of the chord as an *alternate bass note,* abbreviated "Alt."

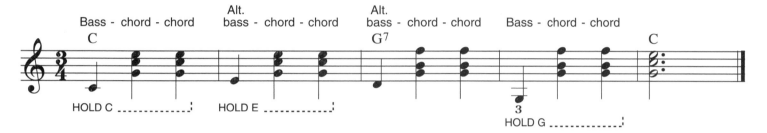

Bonnie Raitt writes and performs music deeply rooted in the American classics of country, blues, and rock. Her style features earthy vocals and superb slide guitar playing, and she has amassed a loyal following since the 1980s.

Photo: © Ken Settle

Chiapanecas (duet)

Learn both parts to this duet. Part 2 uses the bass-chord-chord accompaniment pattern.

Mexican handclapping song

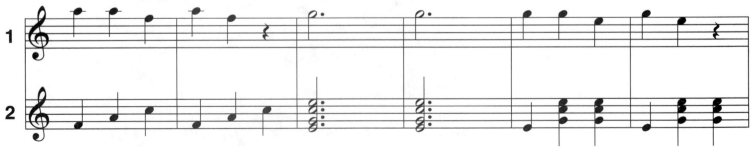

EIGHTH NOTES

Eighth notes are black notes with a flag added to the stem: ♪ or ♪ .

Two or more eighth notes are often written with a *beam:* ♫ or ♫ .

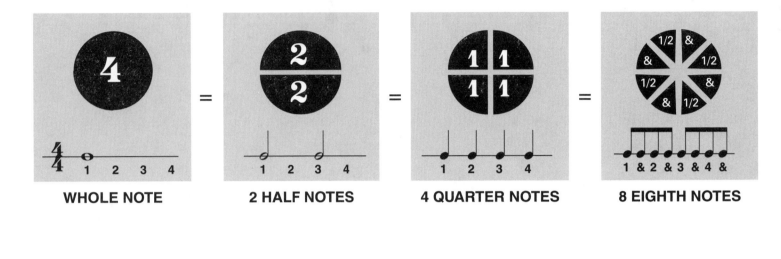

| **WHOLE NOTE** | **2 HALF NOTES** | **4 QUARTER NOTES** | **8 EIGHTH NOTES** |

Use alternating
downstrokes ⊓
and *upstrokes* V
on eighth notes.

COUNT: 1 & 2 & 3 & 4 & 1 & 2 & 3 & 4 &

Jammin' with Eighth Notes

Allegro moderato*

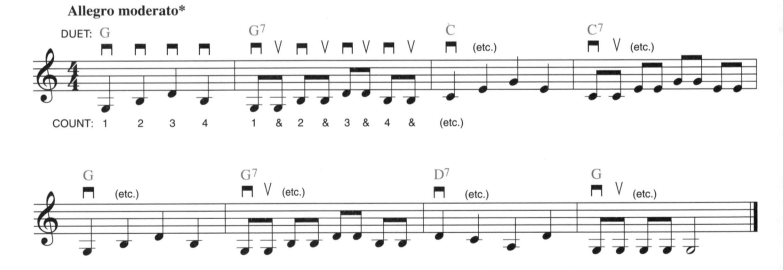

COUNT: 1 2 3 4 1 & 2 & 3 & 4 & (etc.)

* Moderately fast.

Walkin' with Eighths

Blending elements of classical music with characteristics of the blues, Jimmy Page helped shape Led Zeppelin's sound and became one of the true guitar heroes of the 1970s.

Crescendo

Both this sign ——◁ and the word *crescendo* mean to get gradually louder.

Diminuendo

Both this sign ▷—— and the word *diminuendo* mean to get gradually softer.

Pachelbel's Canon

Composer Johann Pachelbel lived from 1653 to 1706. Play this piece as a round, like "Row, Row, Row Your Boat." The first player plays the music as written; the second player begins when the first player gets to [A].

Pachelbel

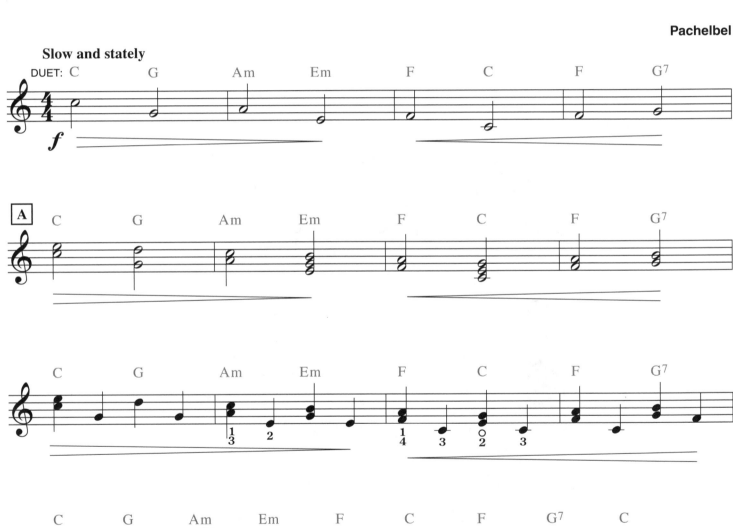

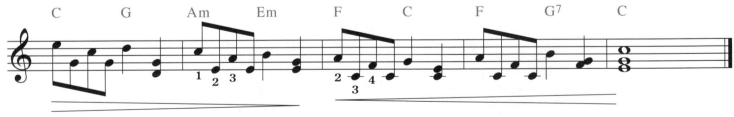

Brian May received his first guitar as a gift for his 7th birthday, and the world of rock is grateful. His guitar playing and vocals contributed to the unique sound of the highly successful group Queen starting in the early 1970s. May was also a successful song-writer, having penned Queen's hit song "We Will Rock You."

SHARPS ♯, FLATS ♭ AND NATURALS ♮

The distance from one fret to the next fret, up or down, is a *half step*.
Two half steps make a *whole step*.

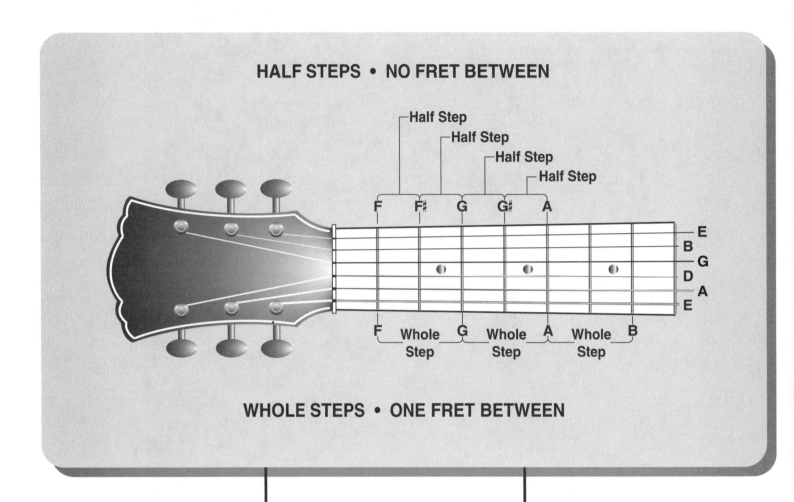

A *sharp* **raises** a note a half step. Play the next fret higher.

A *flat* **lowers** a note a half step. If the note is fingered, play the next fret lower. If the note is open, play the 4th fret of the next lower string, unless that string is G (3rd string)—then play the 3rd fret.

A *natural* **cancels** a previous sharp or flat. A note that is sharp or flat continues to be sharp or flat throughout the same measure unless it is cancelled by a natural. Flats and sharps only last to the end of the measure.

THE CHROMATIC SCALE

The *chromatic scale* is completely made up of half steps. When the chromatic scale
is ascending, it is written with sharps; when it is descending, it is written with flats.

Ascending Chromatic Scale

Descending Chromatic Scale

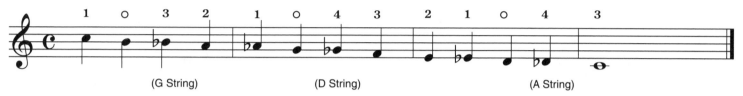

(G String)   (D String)   (A String)

Chromatic Rock

Allegro moderato

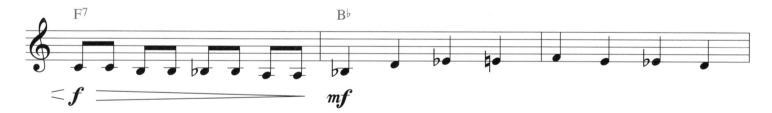

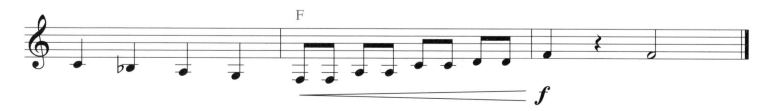

FOUR-STRING D⁷ CHORD

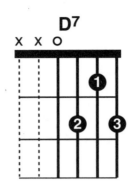

Chord Diagram Review

Chord diagrams show where to place the fingers of your left hand. Strings that are not played are shown with a dashed line. A finger that is to be pressed down is shown as a circle with a number in it. The number indicates which finger to use on that string.

Blues in G

Amazing Grace

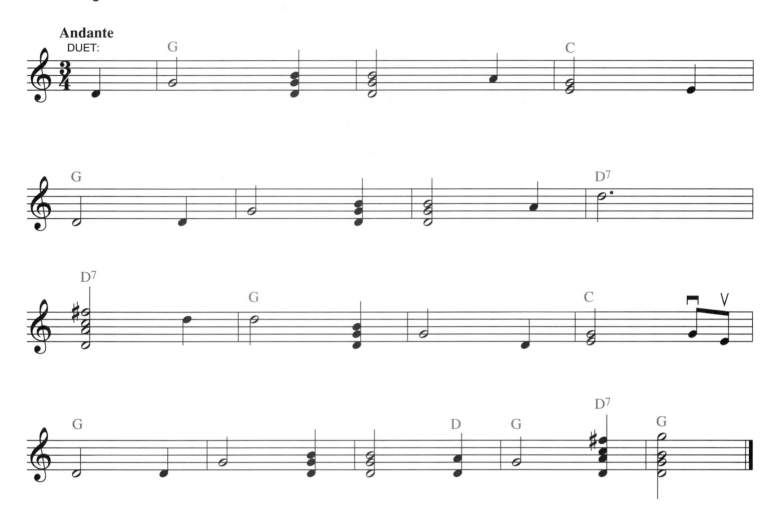

The Who took a larger-than-life approach to rock performance, inspired by the theatrical, powerful compositions of guitarist Pete Townshend. Included among these works is rock's first opera, *Tommy*, which was released in 1969.

Rockin' the Bach

Adapted from a minuet by J.S. Bach

Rockin' Up 'n' Down

Buffalo Gals

Sing "Buffalo Gals" while you play the accompaniment. First, play the
written notes and learn the melody, then play just the chords and sing.

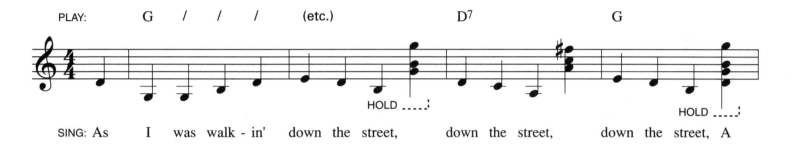

PLAY: G   /   /   /   (etc.)   D7   G

HOLD ....:   HOLD ....:

SING: As   I   was   walk - in'   down   the   street,   down   the   street,   down   the   street, A

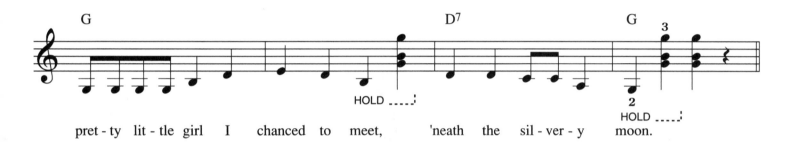

G   D7   G   3

HOLD ....:   2

HOLD ....:

pret - ty   lit - tle   girl   I   chanced   to   meet,   'neath   the   sil - ver - y   moon.

G   D7   G

HOLD ....:   HOLD ....:

Buf - fa - lo   gals,   won't   you   come   out   to - night,   come   out   to - night,   come   out   to - night?

G   D7   G

HOLD ....:   HOLD ....:

Buf - fa - lo   gals,   won't   you   come   out   to - night   and   dance   by   the   light   of   the   moon?

THE MAJOR SCALE

A *major scale* is a succession of eight tones in alphabetical order.
All major scales are built using the same pattern:

WHOLE STEP, WHOLE STEP, HALF STEP, WHOLE STEP, WHOLE STEP, WHOLE STEP, HALF STEP

The major scale has eight notes. The highest note, having the same letter-name as the first note, is called the *octave note.*

C Major Scale

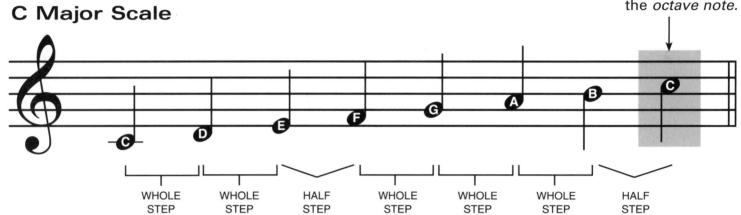

It is easier to visualize whole steps and half steps on a piano keyboard. Notice there is a whole step between all natural notes except from E to F, and B to C.

Whole steps = One key between

Half steps = No key between

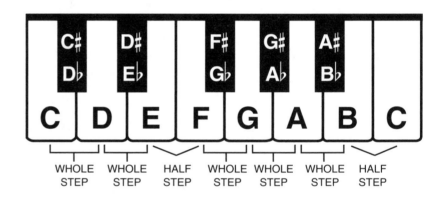

A major scale may be built starting on **any note**, whether natural, sharp or flat.
Using this pattern, write a major scale starting on G.

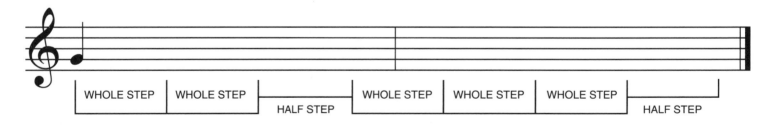

Write a major scale starting on F.

Check: Are the notes in alphabetical order?

KEY SIGNATURES

The Key of C Major

A piece based on the C major scale is in the *key of C major.*
There are no sharps or flats in the C major scale.

The Key of G Major

A piece based on the G major scale is in the *key of G major.* Since F is sharp in the
G scale, every F will be sharp in the key of G major. Instead of writing all the F-sharps
in the piece, the sharp is indicated at the beginning, in the *key signature.* Sharps or
flats shown in the key signature are effective throughout the piece.

The Key of F Major

A piece based on the F major scale is in the *key of F major.*

You should practice the three scales above every day. If you do this, you will
not have any difficulty playing music written in C major, G major or F major.

EIGHTH RESTS

This is an EIGHTH REST.

It means REST for the value of an EIGHTH NOTE.

When eighth notes appear singly, they look like this: ♪ or ♭ .

Single eighth notes are often used with eighth rests: ♪ ↱ .

COUNT: "1   &"

or: "two - 8ths"

Clap or tap the following rhythm:

When an eighth rest follows a fingered note, the sound is cut off by releasing the pressure of the finger on the string. When following an open note, the sound is cut off by touching the string with either a left-hand finger or the heel of the right hand.

Eighth rests may also appear on downbeats. Try to keep an even beat by tapping your foot or silently counting each eighth.

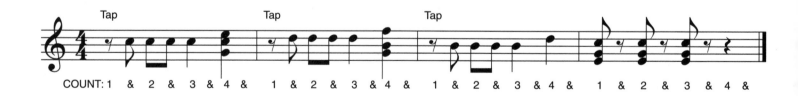

$\frac{2}{4}$ TIME SIGNATURE

Accidentals

If sharps, flats or naturals not shown in the key signature occur in the piece, they are called *accidentals.* Accidentals only last through the measure in which they appear.

Bill Bailey

Moderate ragtime tempo

H. Cannon

68

La Bamba

Allegro moderato

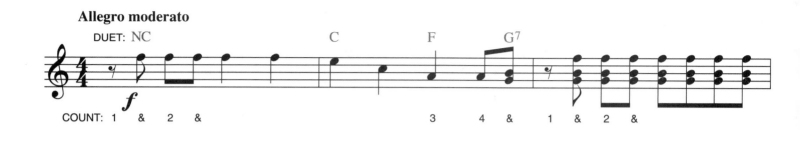

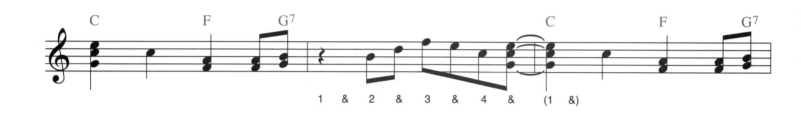

DOTTED QUARTER NOTES

A DOT INCREASES

THE LENGTH OF A NOTE

BY ONE-HALF!

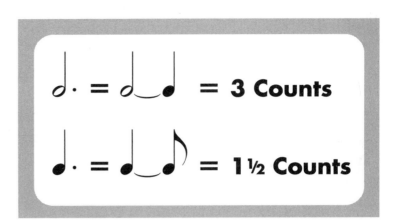

Preparatory Drill

COUNT: 1 & 2 & 3 & 4 &   1 & 2 & 3 & 4 &   1 & 2 & 3 & 4 &

The only difference in the following two measures and those directly above them is the way they are written. They should sound the SAME.

COUNT: 1 & 2 & 3 & 4 &   1 & 2 & 3 & 4 &

Auld Lang Syne

Hava Nagila

Israeli folk song

Brightly

DUET: B⁷

Still sharp

p - mf (Play *p* the 1st time, *mf* the 2nd time.)

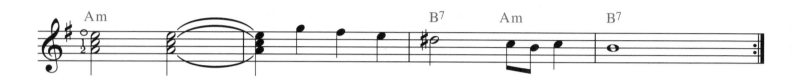

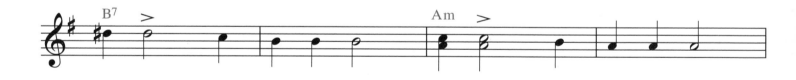

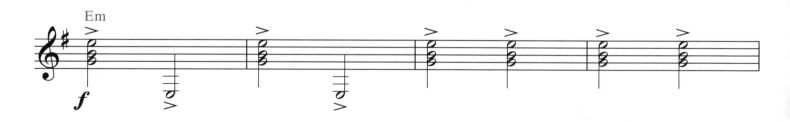

* > = *Accent.* Play the note a little louder.

Eric Clapton is a rock icon whose playing has been studied and copied for years. Like other guitar greats of his generation, he was heavily influenced by the blues, and this is evident in most of his recordings spanning from the early projects with the Yardbirds and Cream to his successful solo work.

KEY OF C MAJOR

C Major Scale

Three Chords in C Major

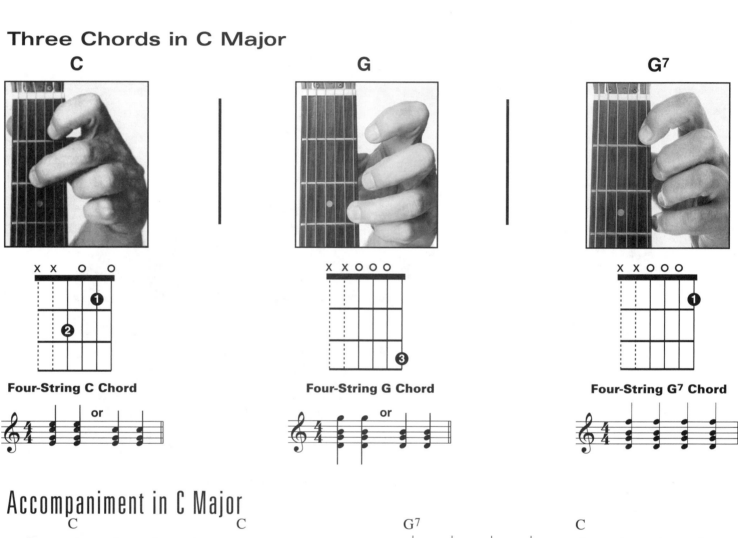

C   **G**   **G⁷**

Four-String C Chord   Four-String G Chord   Four-String G⁷ Chord

Accompaniment in C Major

TWO-OCTAVE C MAJOR SCALE

The C major scale can be extended to a full two octaves by adding high A, high B and high C.

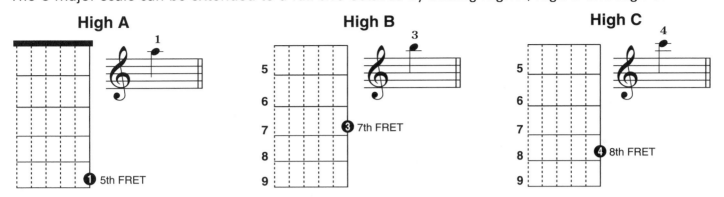

Ascending Two-Octave C Major Scale

Shift the hand up the neck

Descending Two-Octave C Major Scale

Shift down the neck

Practice these scales every day. Make every effort to play the notes under the brackets as smoothly as possible.

Joy to the World

Handel

THREE-STRING F MINOR CHORD

The F minor chord is a new chord that requires putting your first finger across three strings. Press hard near (but not on) the 1st fret.

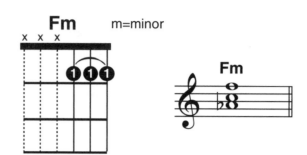

Home on the Range

American cowboy song

Oh, give me a home where the buf - fa - lo roam, where the

deer and the an - te - lope play. Where

sel - dom is heard a dis - cour - ag - ing word, and the

* A wavy line ⌇ in front of a chord means to run the pick across the strings more slowly to obtain a rippling, harp-like sound. The technical term for creating this effect is the Italian word *arpeggiando,* often abbreviated "arp."

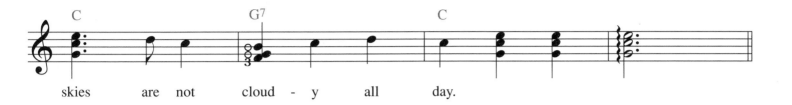

skies   are   not   cloud - y   all   day.

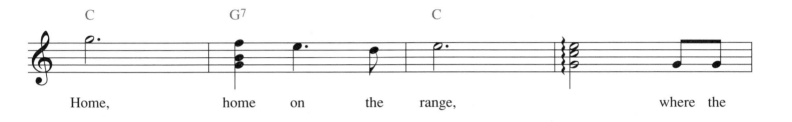

Home,   home   on   the   range,   where the

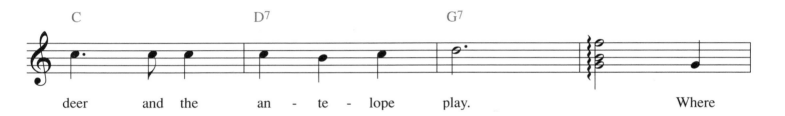

deer   and   the   an - te - lope   play.   Where

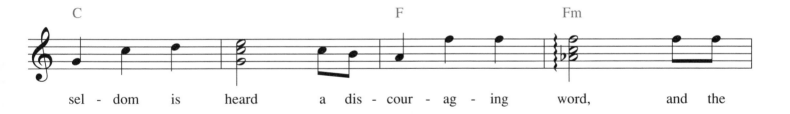

sel - dom   is   heard   a   dis - cour - ag - ing   word,   and the

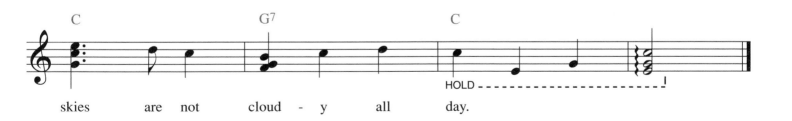

skies   are   not   cloud - y   all   day.

76

Variation on Little Brown Jug

This tune will help you develop your technique for playing
repeated notes. Pay attention to the picking directions.

CUT TIME

This symbol 𝄵 stands for *cut time,* which means the time values of the notes are cut
in half. The half note receives one beat, and the quarter note receives one-half beat.

Variation on Jim Crack Corn

BASS MELODY WITH CHORD ACCOMPANIMENT

When the melody of a song is in the bass notes and there is chord accompaniment, the melody part is written with the stems pointing down and the chords with stems pointing up. In the example below, the bass melody begins on the first beat and is held for three beats. The quarter rest shows that the chord accompaniment begins on the second beat.

Meet Me in St. Louis, Louis

A.B. Sterling,
Kerry Mills

an - y place but there. We will

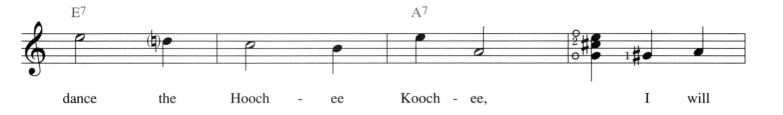

dance the Hooch - ee Kooch - ee, I will

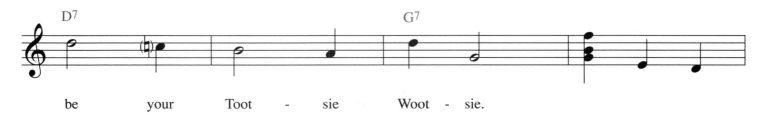

be your Toot - sie Woot - sie.

Meet me in St. Lou - is, Lou - is,

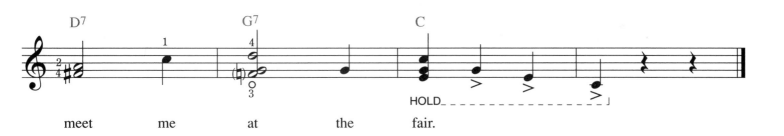

HOLD_ _ _ _ _ _ _ _ _ _ _ _ _ _ ⌟

meet me at the fair.

KEY OF G MAJOR

As you learned on page 62, the key signature of one sharp indicates the key of G major. All F's are played as F-sharp unless otherwise indicated by a natural sign.

G Major Scale

The Three Principal Chords in G Major

The three principal (most commonly used) chords in any key are built on the first, fourth and fifth notes of the scale. The chord built on the fifth note usually adds a seventh tone to it. The chords are known as 1, 4, 5(7) chords and are sometimes indicated by Roman numerals: I, IV, V7. The three principal chords in the key of G major are G, C and D7.

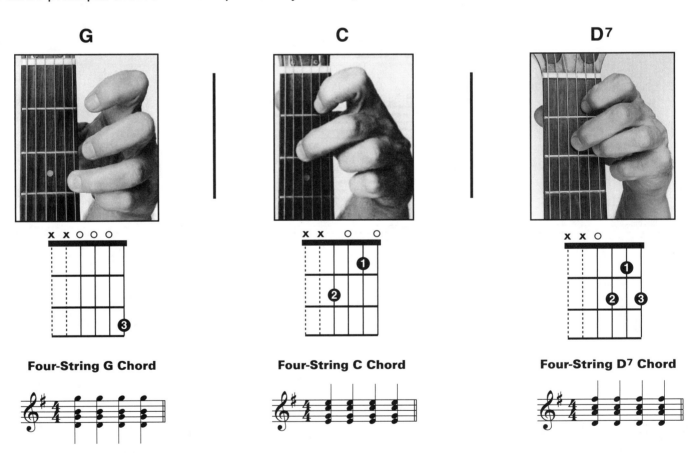

G   C   D7

Four-String G Chord   **Four-String C Chord**   **Four-String D7 Chord**

Tiritomba

First, learn the melody of this song. It's in the key of G and makes use of many repeated notes. Then, play along with the DVD or have your teacher or a friend play the melody while you strum the chords, four to each measure.

Rakes of Mallow

The Old Chisholm Trail (duet)

Learn both parts of this song, then play it as a duet with a friend, your teacher or the DVD.
Finally, sing the melody (the top staff) while playing the accompaniment (the bottom staff).

A natural-born showman, Garth Brooks is noted for his wonderful live performances and a style that ranges from honky-tonk to a sound that encompasses '70s-oriented soft rock.

Ain't Gonna Rain (duet)

Learn both parts of this song, then play it as a duet with a friend, your teacher or the DVD.
Finally, sing the melody (the top staff) while playing the accompaniment (the bottom staff).

It ain't gon - na rain, it ain't gon - na snow, it ain't gon - na rain no more; Come on ev - 'ry - bod - y now, Ain't gon - na rain no more.

With a unique sound and brilliant songwriting ability, the 1960s supergroup The Beatles attained a level of popularity more immense than any other band. The guitar skills of John Lennon and George Harrison contributed significantly to the group's distinctive sound. The combination of Lennon's driving rhythm guitar, Harrison's infectious leads, the melodic bass lines of Paul McCartney, and Ringo Starr's understated drumming created unstoppable hits that are still popular today.

This Land Is Your Land (duet or trio)

Learn both parts of this classic song.

Woody Guthrie

Photo: © Bettmann/CORBIS

Performer and songwriter Woody Guthrie is an American folk hero. A series of hardships among his early family experiences lead to life-long sympathies for the poor and downtrodden that were frequently expressed in his music. Guthrie started playing guitar in 1926, but didn't realize a life as a performer until 1938 when he hosted a radio show. He eventually went on to record albums and wrote many popular folk songs including "This Land Is Your Land."

Margarita

March tempo

Shortnin' Bread

This tune will help you develop your technique for playing skips.

Moderato

Red River Valley (duet)

First, learn both parts of this song, then play it as a duet with a friend, your teacher or the DVD.
Finally, sing the melody (the top staff) while playing the accompaniment (the bottom staff).

America (duet)

Learn both parts.

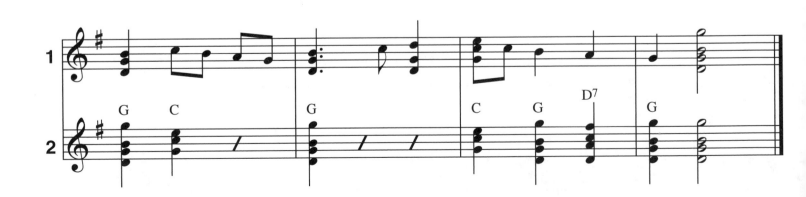

KEY OF A MINOR

For every major key there is a minor key called the *relative minor* that has the same key signature. The keys of A minor and C major are relative keys because they have the same key signature (no sharps, no flats). The relative minor scale is built on the sixth tone of the major scale. Chords are built on the harmonic minor scale, which has its seventh step *augmented* (raised a half step).

Two-Octave A Harmonic Minor Scale

The Three Principal Chords in A Minor

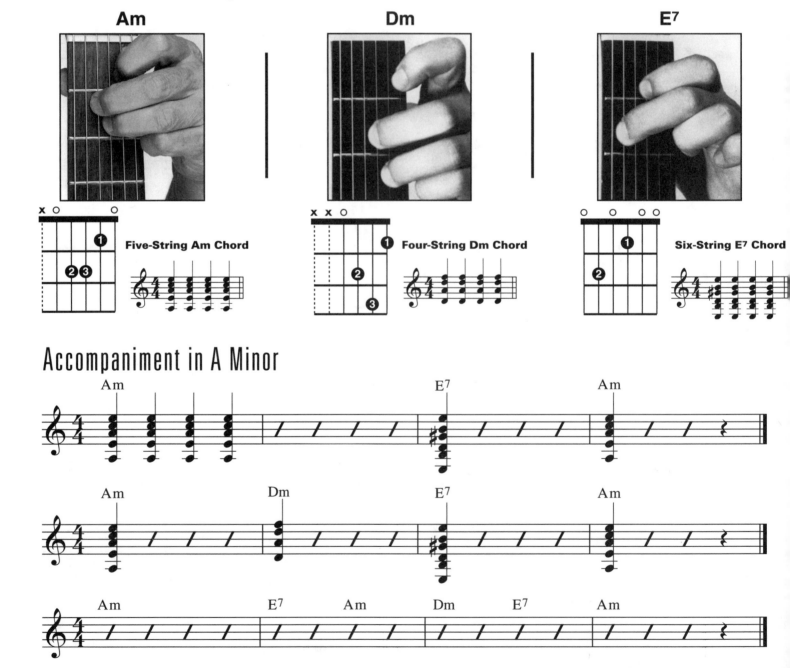

Accompaniment in A Minor

Waves of the Danube

*D.C. stands for *Da Capo*, which is Italian for "the head" or "the beginning." Play from the beginning to the ⊕, then skip directly to the *coda* (the last two measures).

Four-String F Chord

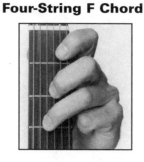
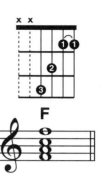

FOUR-STRING F CHORD

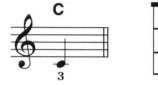

Bass-Chord Accompaniment in the Key of C Major

The three principal chords in the key of C major are C, F and G⁷. Chord accompaniment is considerably improved by replacing the first chord of each measure with a bass note. The simplest bass note is the *root* (the letter-name) of the chord.

With the C (I) chord, play the bass note C.

With the F (IV) chord, play the bass note F.

With the G or G⁷ (V⁷) chord, play the bass note G.

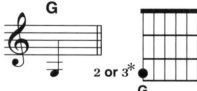

* Some guitarists use the left thumb to finger bass notes on the low E string when followed by a chord. You can also try this technique. Use whichever is most comfortable for you.

Bass-Chord-Chord-Chord

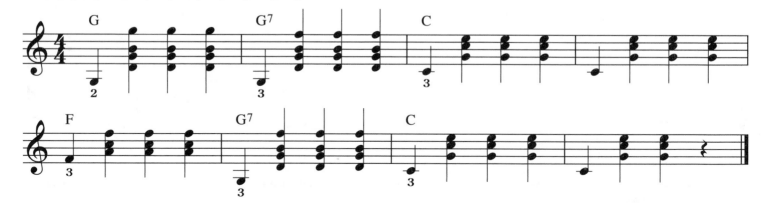

The Yellow Rose of Texas (duet)

Moderato

She's my Rose - bud, she's my Dar - lin'! My love is sweet and true! I

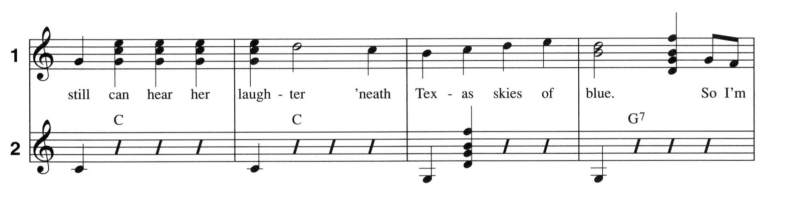

still can hear her laugh - ter 'neath Tex - as skies of blue. So I'm

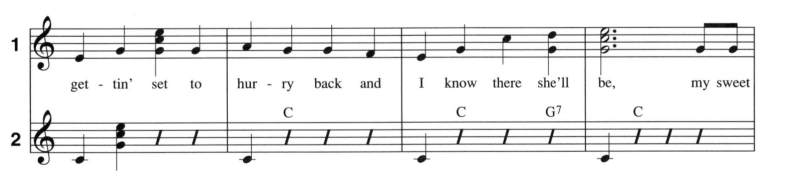

get - tin' set to hur - ry back and I know there she'll be, my sweet

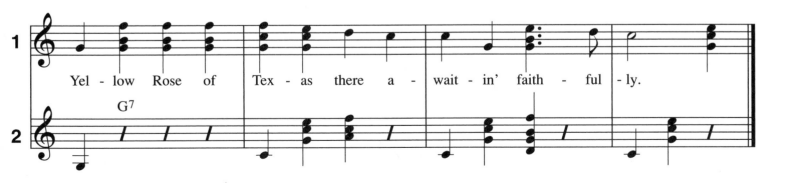

Yel - low Rose of Tex - as there a - wait - in' faith - ful - ly.

CHORD THEORY
Intervals

Play any note on the guitar, then play a note one fret above it. The distance between these two notes is a *half step.* Play another note followed by a note two frets above it. The distance between these two notes is a *whole step* (two half steps). The distance between any two notes is referred to as an *interval*.

In the example of the C major scale below, the letter names are shown above the notes and the *scale degrees* (numbers) of the notes are written below. Notice that C is the first degree of the scale, D is the second, etc.

The name of an interval is determined by counting the number of scale degrees from one note to the next. For example, an interval of a 3rd, starting on C, would be determined by counting up three scale degrees, or C-D-E (1-2-3). C to E is a 3rd. An interval of a 4th, starting on C, would be determined by counting up four scale degrees, or C-D-E-F (1-2-3-4). C to F is a 4th.

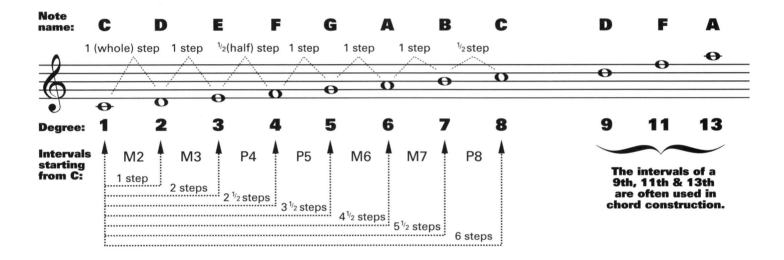

Intervals are not only labeled by the distance between scale degrees, but by the *quality* of the interval. An interval's quality is determined by counting the number of whole steps and half steps between the two notes of an interval. For example, C to E is a 3rd. C to E is also a major third because there are 2 whole steps between C and E. Likewise, C to E♭ is a 3rd. C to E♭ is also a minor third because there are 1½ steps between C and E♭. There are five qualities used to describe intervals: *major, minor, perfect, diminished,* and *augmented*.

M = Major
m = Minor
P = Perfect

o = Diminished (dim)
+ = Augmented (aug)

Particular intervals are associated with certain qualities:

2nds, 9ths	= **Major, Minor & Augmented**
3rds, 6ths, 13ths	= **Major, Minor, Augmented & Diminished**
4ths, 5ths, 11ths	= **Perfect, Augmented & Diminished**
7ths	= **Major, Minor & Diminished**

When a *major* interval is made **smaller** by a half step it becomes a *minor* interval.

When a *minor* interval is made **larger** by a half step it becomes a *major* interval.

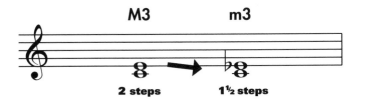

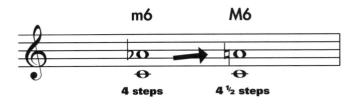

When a *minor* or *perfect* interval is made **smaller** by a half step it becomes a *diminished* interval.

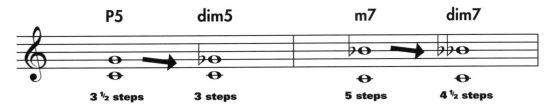

When a *major* or *perfect* interval is made **larger** by a half step it becomes an *augmented* interval.

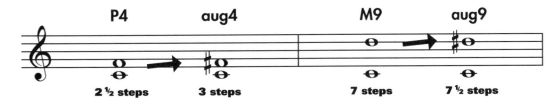

Below is a table of intervals starting on the note C. Notice that some intervals are labeled enharmonic, which means that they are written differently but sound the same (see **aug2** & **m3**).

TABLE OF INTERVALS

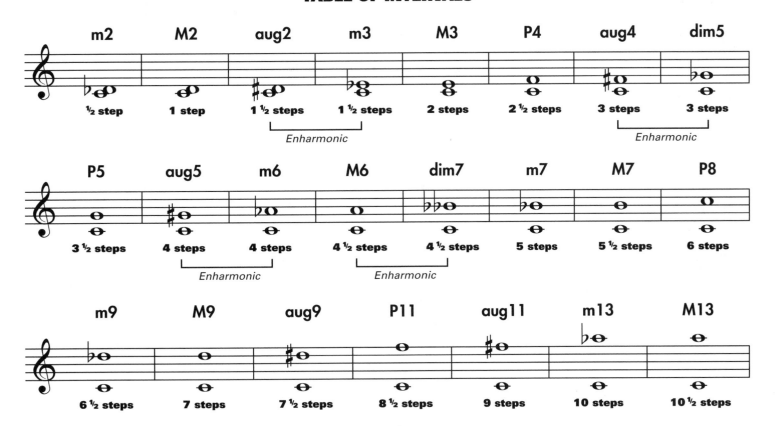

Basic Triads

Two or more notes played together is called a *chord*. Most commonly, a chord will consist of three or more notes. A three-note chord is called a *triad*. The *root* of a triad (or any other chord) is the note from which a chord is constructed. The relationship of the intervals from the root to the other notes of a chord determines the chord *type*. Triads are most frequently identified as one of four chord types: *major*, *minor*, *diminished* and *augmented*.

All chord types can be identified by the intervals used to create the chord. For example, the C major triad is built beginning with C as the root, adding a major 3rd (E) and adding a perfect 5th (G). All major triads contain a root, M3 and P5.

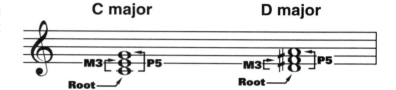

Minor triads contain a root, minor 3rd and perfect 5th. (An easier way to build a minor triad is to simply lower the 3rd of a major triad.) All minor triads contain a root, m3 and P5.

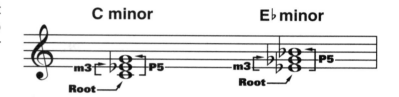

Diminished triads contain a root, minor 3rd and diminished 5th. If the perfect 5th of a minor triad is made smaller by a half step (to become a diminished 5th), the result is a diminished triad. All diminished triads contain a root, m3 and dim5.

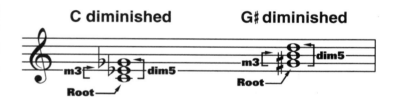

Augmented triads contain a root, major 3rd and augmented 5th. If the perfect 5th of a major triad is made larger by a half step (to become an augmented 5th), the result is an augmented triad. All augmented triads contain a root, M3 and aug5.

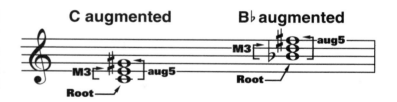

An important concept to remember about chords is that the bottom note of a chord will not always be the root. If the root of a triad, for instance, is moved above the 5th so that the 3rd is the bottom note of the chord, it is said to be in the *first inversion*. If the root and 3rd are moved above the 5th, the chord is in the *second inversion*. The number of inversions that a chord can have is related to the number of notes in the chord: a three-note chord can have two inversions, a four-note chord can have three inversions, etc.

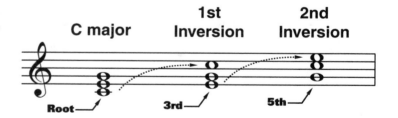

Building Chords

By using the four chord types as basic building blocks, it is possible to create a variety of chords by adding 6ths, 7ths, 9ths, 11ths, etc. The following are examples of some of the many variations.

*The *suspended fourth* chord does not contain a third. An assumption is made that the 4th degree of the chord will harmonically be inclined to *resolve* to the 3rd degree. In other words, the 4th is *suspended* until it moves to the 3rd.

100

Thus far, the examples provided to illustrate intervals and chord construction have been based on C. Until familiarity with chords is achieved, the C chord examples on the previous page can serve as a reference guide when building chords based on other notes: For instance, locate C7(♭9). To construct a G7(♭9) chord, first determine what intervals are contained in C7(♭9), then follow the steps outlined below.

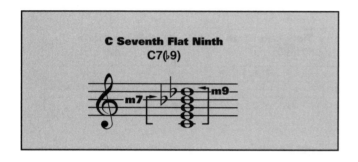

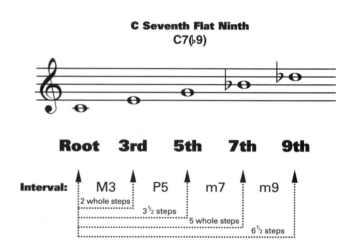

- Determine the *root* of the chord. A chord is always named for its root—in this instance, G is the root of G7(♭9).

- Count *letter names* up from the *letter name of the root* (G), as was done when building intervals on page 96, to determine the intervals of the chord. Therefore, counting three letter names up from G to B (G-A-B, 1-2-3) is a 3rd, G to D (G-A-B-C-D) is a 5th, G to F is a 7th, and G to A is a 9th.

- Determine the *quality* of the intervals by counting whole steps and half steps up from the root; G to B (2 whole steps) is a major 3rd, G to D (3½ steps) is a perfect 5th, G to F (5 whole steps) is a minor 7th, and G to A♭ (6½ steps) is a minor 9th.

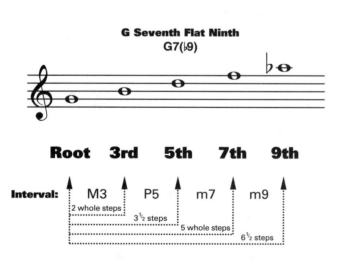

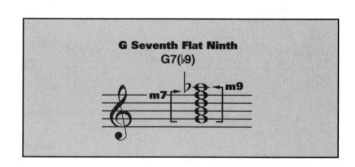

Follow this general guideline for determining the notes of any chord. As interval and chord construction become more familiar to the beginning guitarist, it will become possible to create original fingerings on the guitar. Experimentation is suggested.

The Circle of Fifths

The *circle of fifths* will help to clarify which chords are enharmonic equivalents (notice that *chords* can be written enharmonically as well as *notes*). The circle of fifths also serves as a quick reference guide to the relationship of the keys and how key signatures can be figured out in a logical manner. Clockwise movement (up a P5) provides all of the sharp keys by adding one sharp to the key signature progressively. Counter-clockwise (down a P5) provides the flat keys by adding one flat similarly.

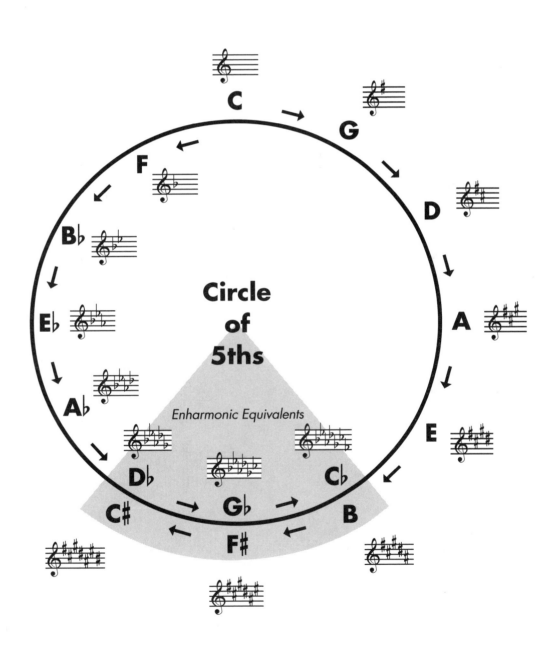

Chord Symbol Variations

Chord symbols are a form of musical shorthand providing the guitarist with as much information about a chord as quickly as possible. The intent of using chord symbols is to convey enough information to recognize the chord yet not so much as to confuse the meaning of the symbol. Since chord symbols are not universally standardized, they are often written in many different ways—some are understandable, others are confusing. To illustrate this point, below is a listing of some of the ways copyists, composers and arrangers have created variations on the more common chord symbols.

C	**Csus**	**C($\flat$5)**	**C(add9)**	**C5**	**Cm**
C major	Csus4	C-5	C(9)	C(no3)	Cmin
Cmaj	C(addF)	C(5-)	C(add2)	C(omit3)	Cmi
CM	C4	C($\sharp$4)	C(+9)		C-
			C(+D)		

C+	**C°**	**C6**	**C6/9**	**Cm6/9**	**Cm6**
C+5	Cdim	Cmaj6	C6(add9)	C-6/9	C-6
Caug	Cdim7	C(addA)	C6(addD)	Cm6(+9)	Cm(addA)
Caug5	C7dim	C(A)	C9(no7)	Cm6(add9)	Cm(+6)
C($\sharp$5)			C9/6	Cm6(+D)	

C7	**C7sus**	**Cm7**	**Cm7($\flat$5)**	**C7+**	**C7($\flat$5)**
C(addB$\flat$)	C7sus4	Cmi7	Cmi7-5	C7+5	C7-5
C$\overline{7}$	Csus7	Cmin7	C-7(5-)	C7aug	C7(5-)
C(-7)	C7(+4)	C-7	C$\varnothing$	C7aug5	C$\overline{7}$-5
C(+7)		C7mi	C ½dim	C7($\sharp$5)	C7($\sharp$4)

Cmaj7	**Cmaj7($\flat$5)**	**Cm(maj7)**	**C7($\flat$9)**	**C7($\sharp$9)**	**C7+($\flat$9)**
Cma7	Cmaj7(-5)	C-maj7	C7(-9)	C7(+9)	Caug7-9
C$\overline{7}$	C$\overline{7}$(-5)	C-$\overline{7}$	C9$\flat$	C9$\sharp$	C+7($\flat$9)
C$\triangle$	C$\triangle$($\flat$5)	Cmi$\overline{7}$	C9-	C9+	C+9$\flat$
C$\triangle$7					C7+(-9)

Cm9	**C9**	**C9+**	**C9($\flat$5)**	**Cmaj9**	**C9($\sharp$11)**
Cm7(9)	C$\overline{7}^{9}$	C9(+5)	C9(-5)	C$\overline{7}$(9)	C9(+11)
Cm7(+9)	C7add9	Caug9	C7$^{9}_{-5}$	C$\overline{7}$(+9)	C($\sharp$11)
C-9	C7(addD)	C($\sharp$9$\sharp$5)	C9(5$\flat$)	C9(maj7)	C11+
Cmi7(9+)	C7(+9)	C+9		C$\overline{9}$	C11$\sharp$

Cm9(maj7)	**C11**	**Cm11**	**C13**	**C13($\flat$9)**	**C13($\genfrac{}{}{0pt}{}{\flat 9}{\flat 5}$)**
C-9($\sharp$7)	C9(11)	C-11	C9addA	C13(-9)	C13(-9-5)
C(-9)$\overline{7}$	C9addF	Cm($\flat$11)	C9(6)	C$^{13}_{\flat 9}$	C($\flat$9$\flat$5)addA
Cmi9($\sharp$7)	C9+11	Cmi7$^{11}_{9}$	C7addA	C($\flat$9)addA	
	C7$^{9}_{11}$	C-7($^{9}_{11}$)	C7+A		

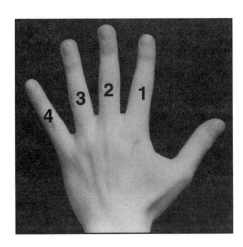

Reading Chords

Guitar chord frames are diagrams that contain all the information necessary to play a particular chord. The fingerings, note names and position of the chord on the neck are all provided on the chord frame (see below). The photograph at left shows which finger number corresponds to which finger.

Choose chord positions that require the least motion from one chord to the next; select fingerings that are in approximately the same location on the guitar neck. This will provide smoother and more comfortable transitions between chords in a progression.

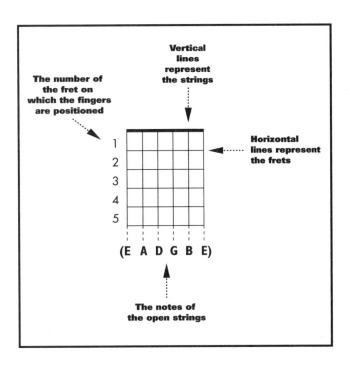

Vertical lines represent the strings

The number of the fret on which the fingers are positioned

Horizontal lines represent the frets

(E A D G B E)

The notes of the open strings

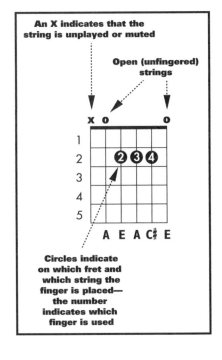

An X indicates that the string is unplayed or muted

Open (unfingered) strings

A E A C♯ E

Circles indicate on which fret and which string the finger is placed—the number indicates which finger is used

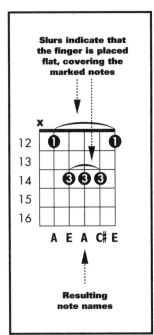

Slurs indicate that the finger is placed flat, covering the marked notes

A E A C♯ E

Resulting note names

A

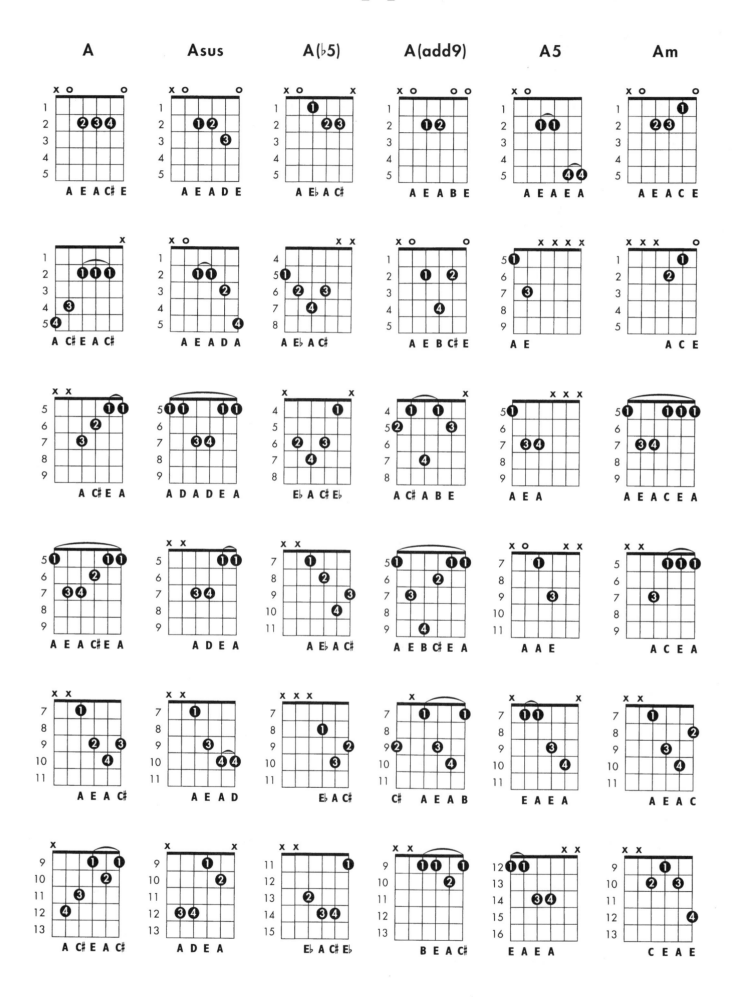

A

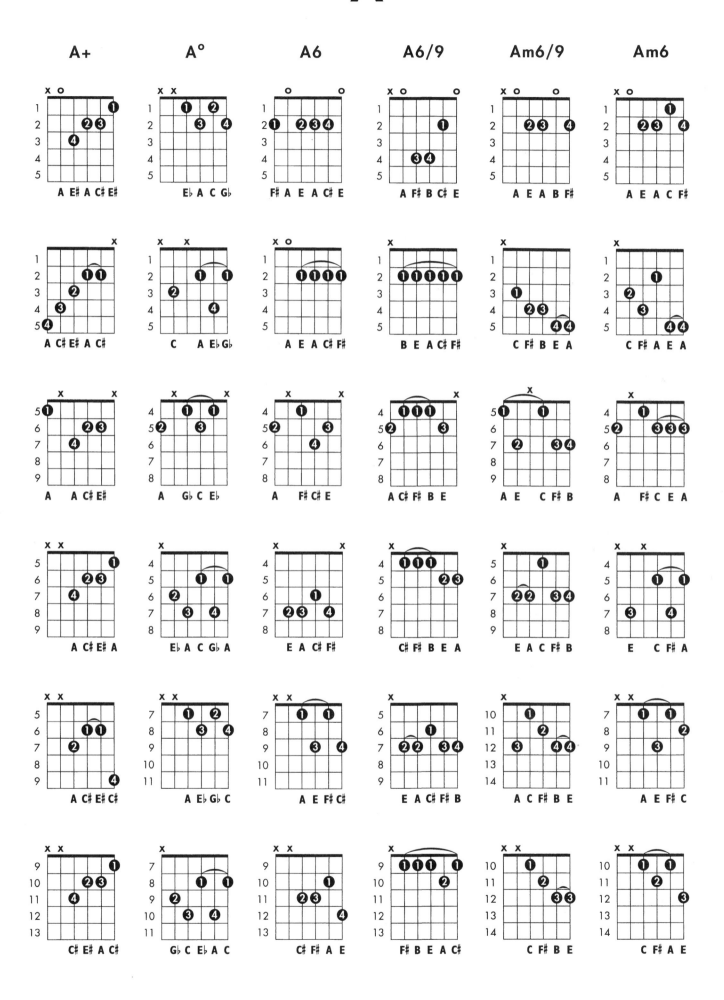

A

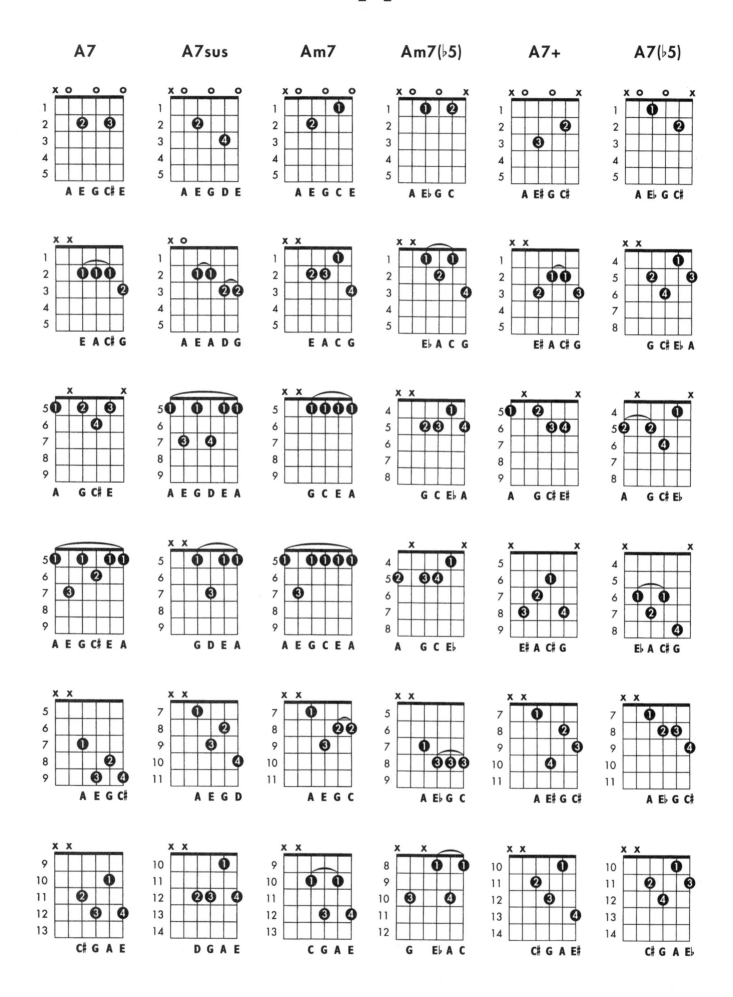

A

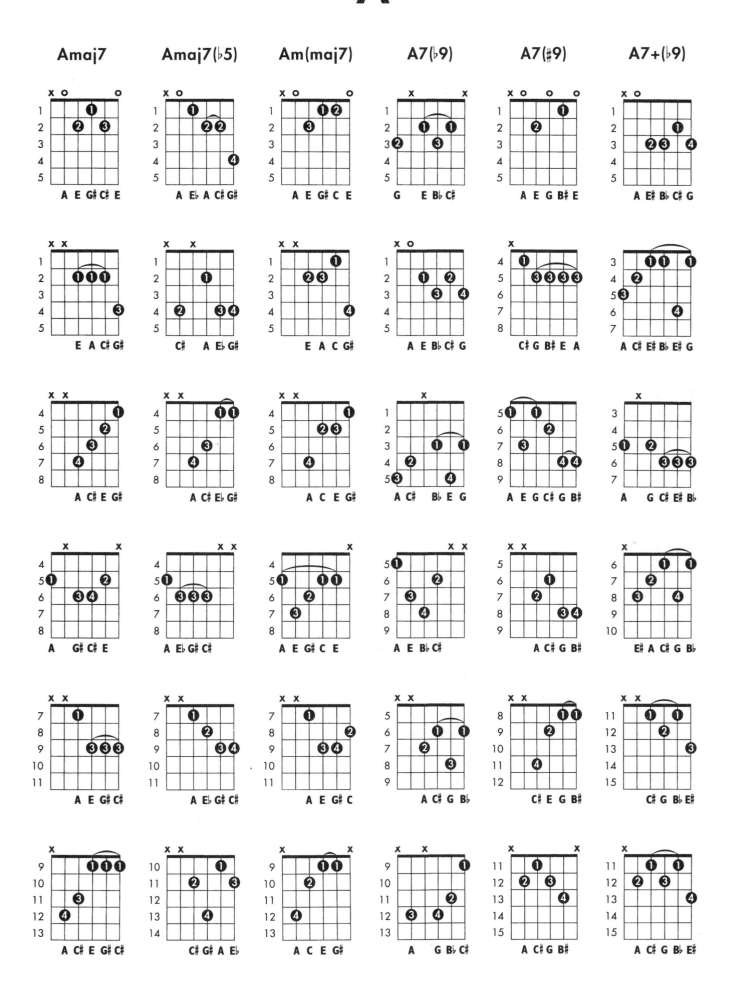

B♭

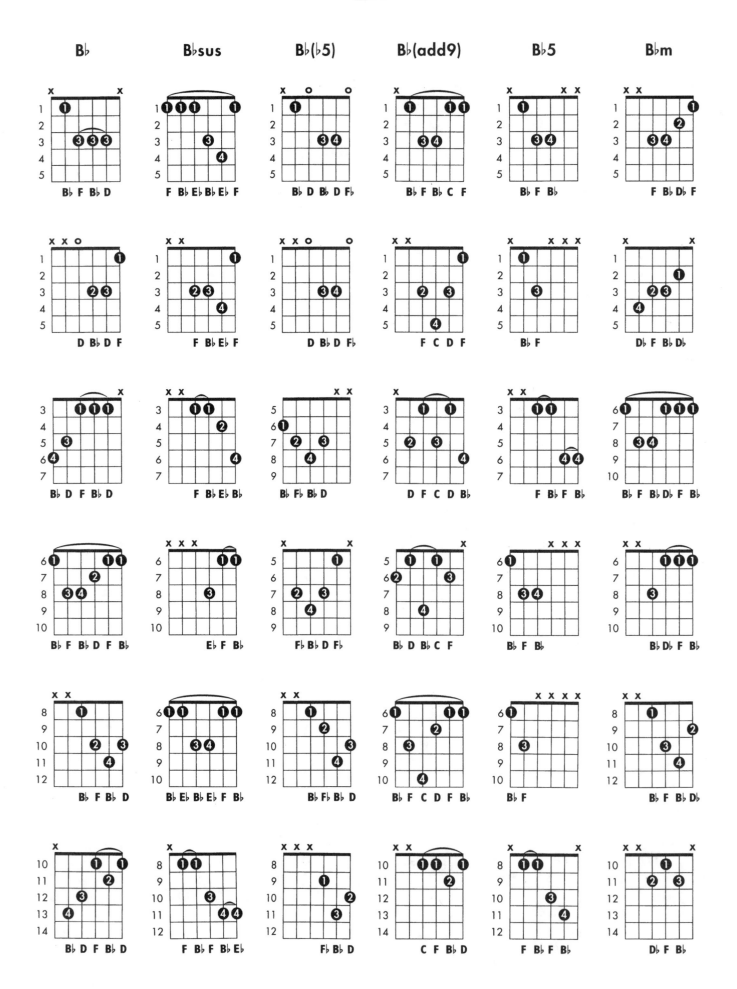

B♭

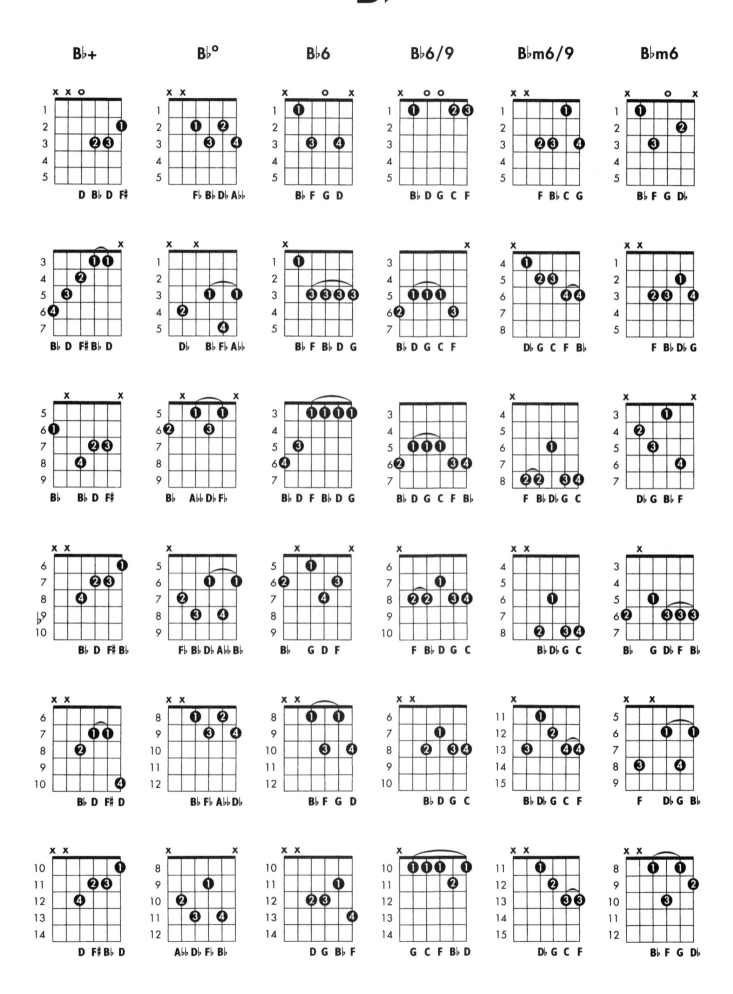

B♭

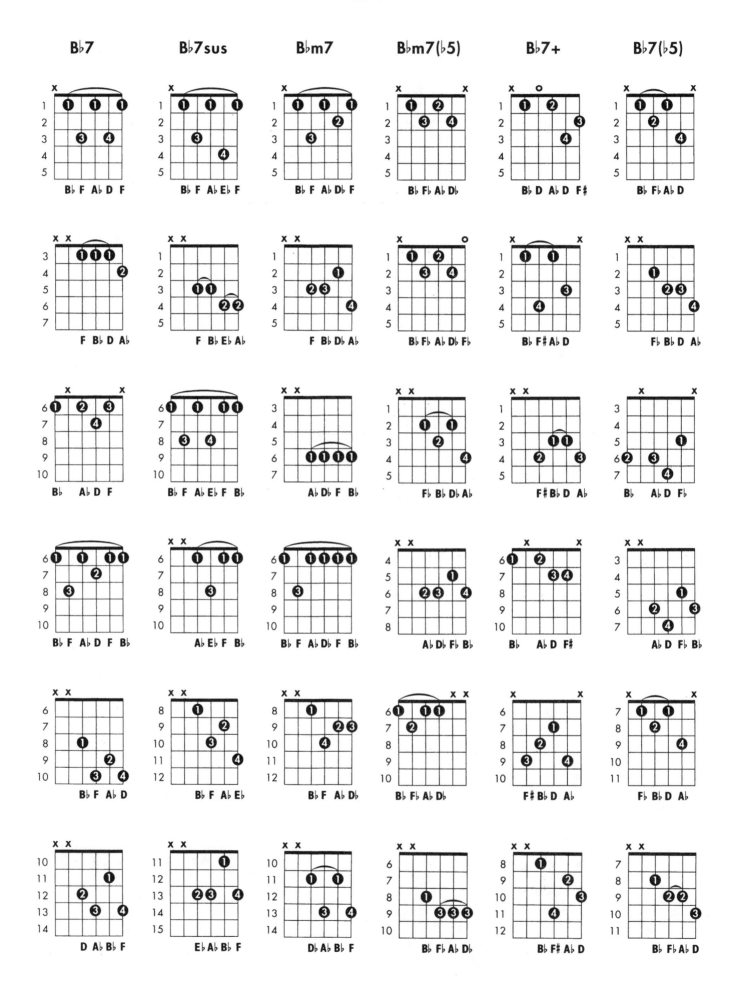

B♭

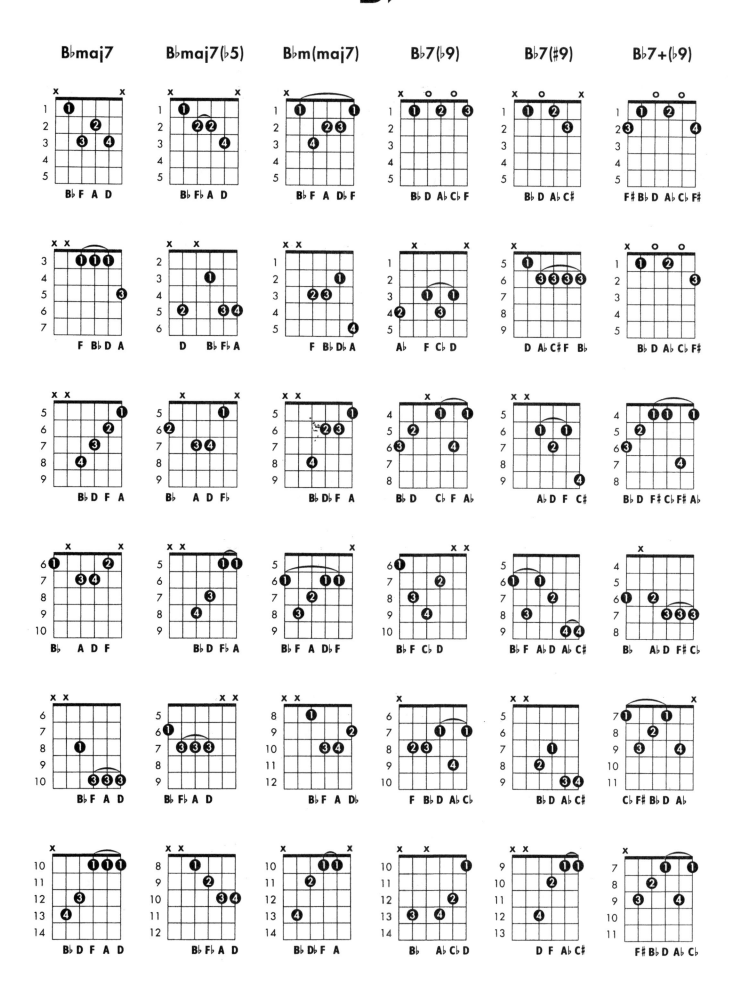

B

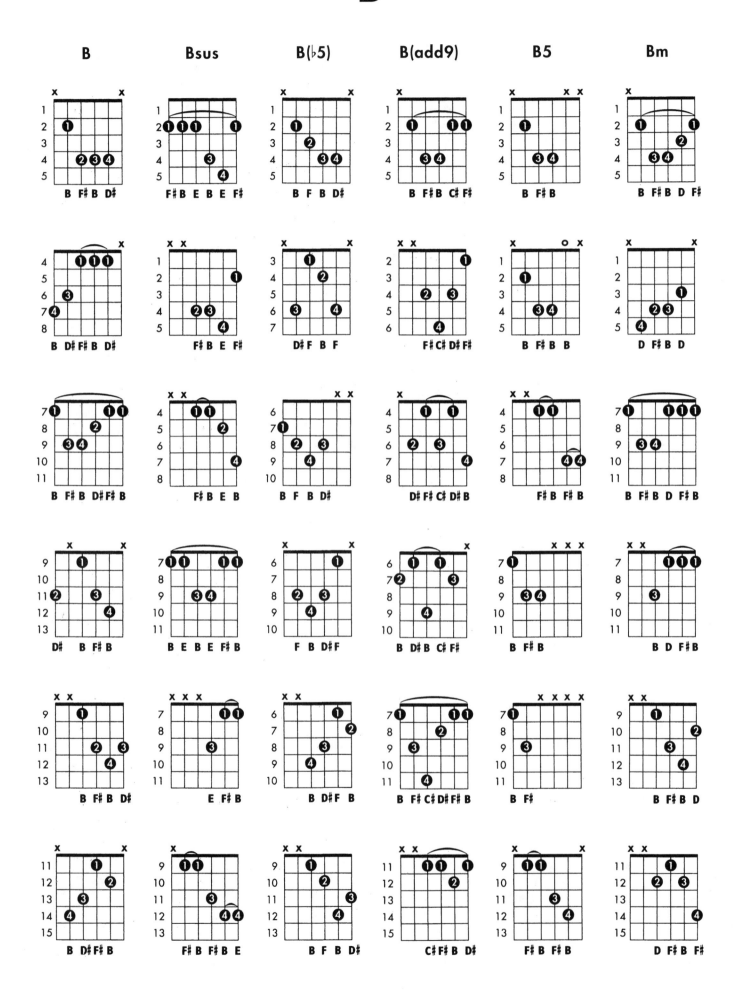

B

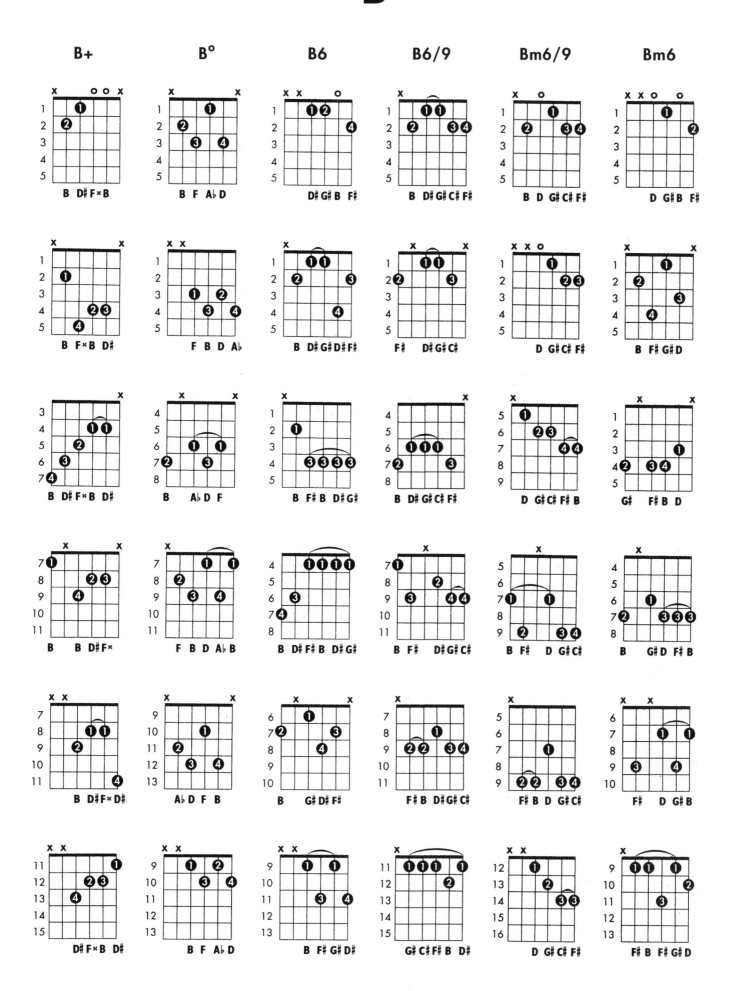

B

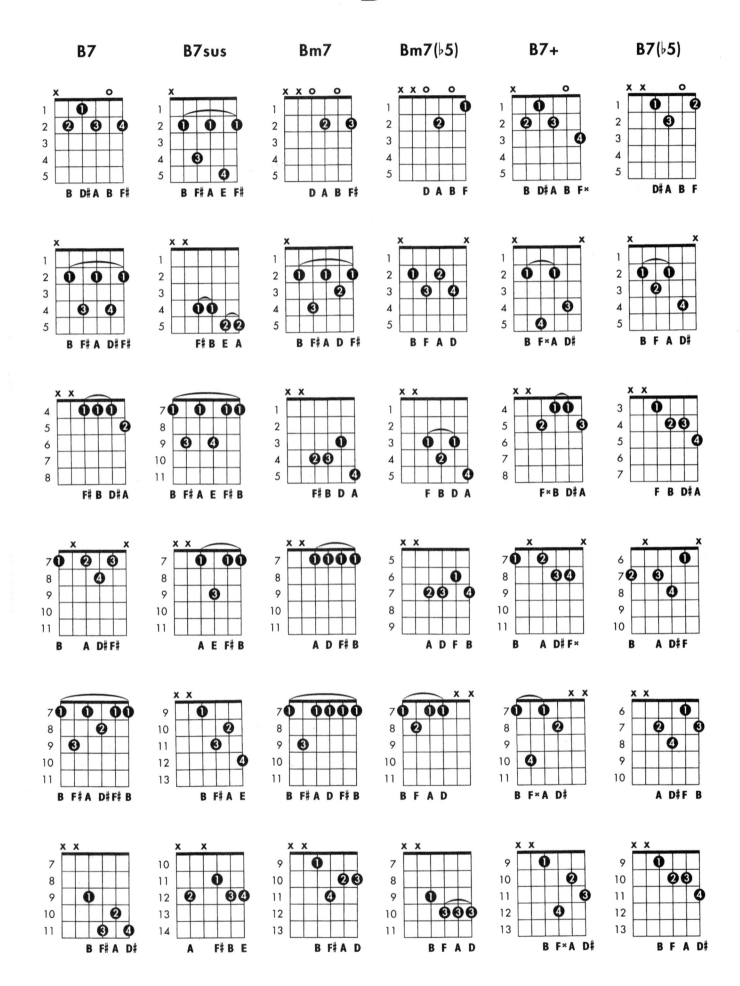

B

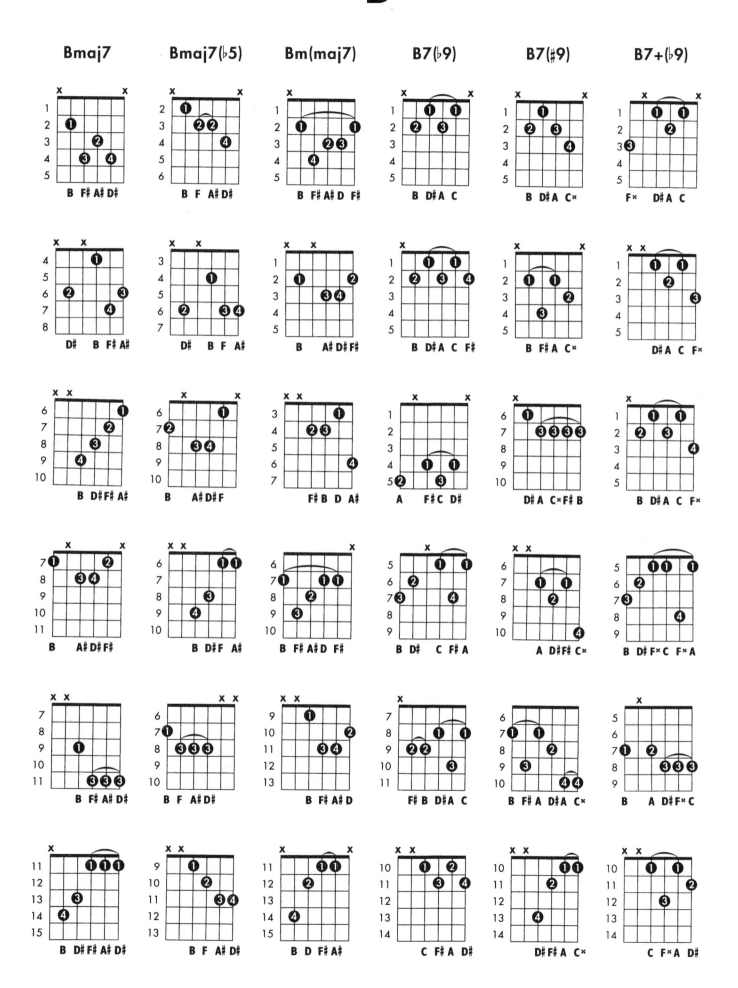

C

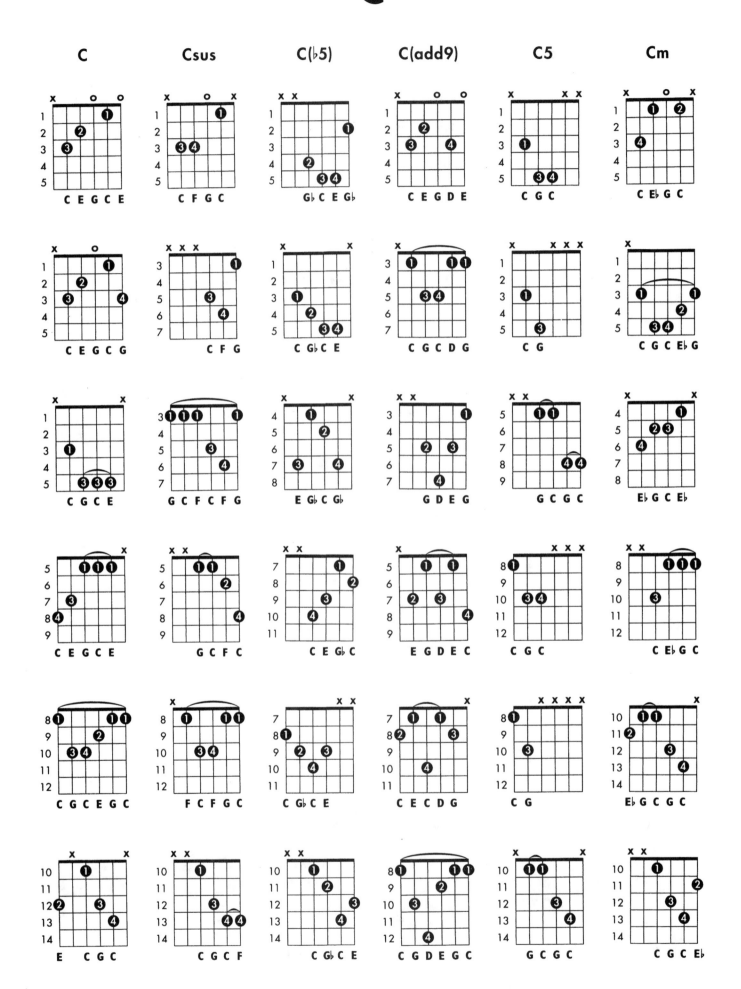

C

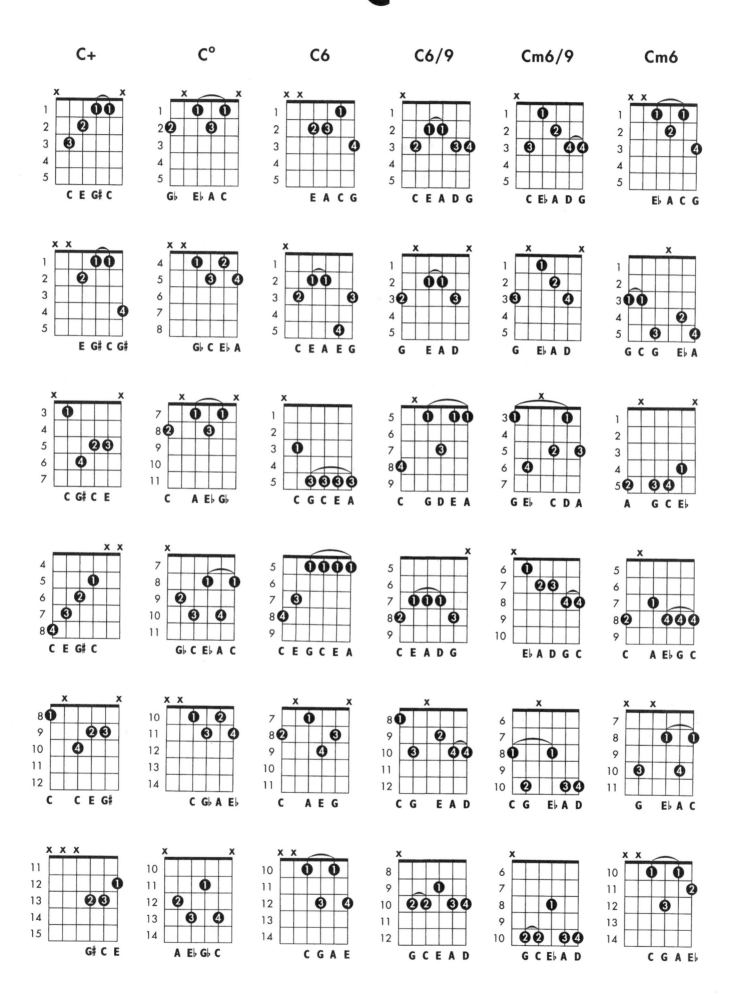

C

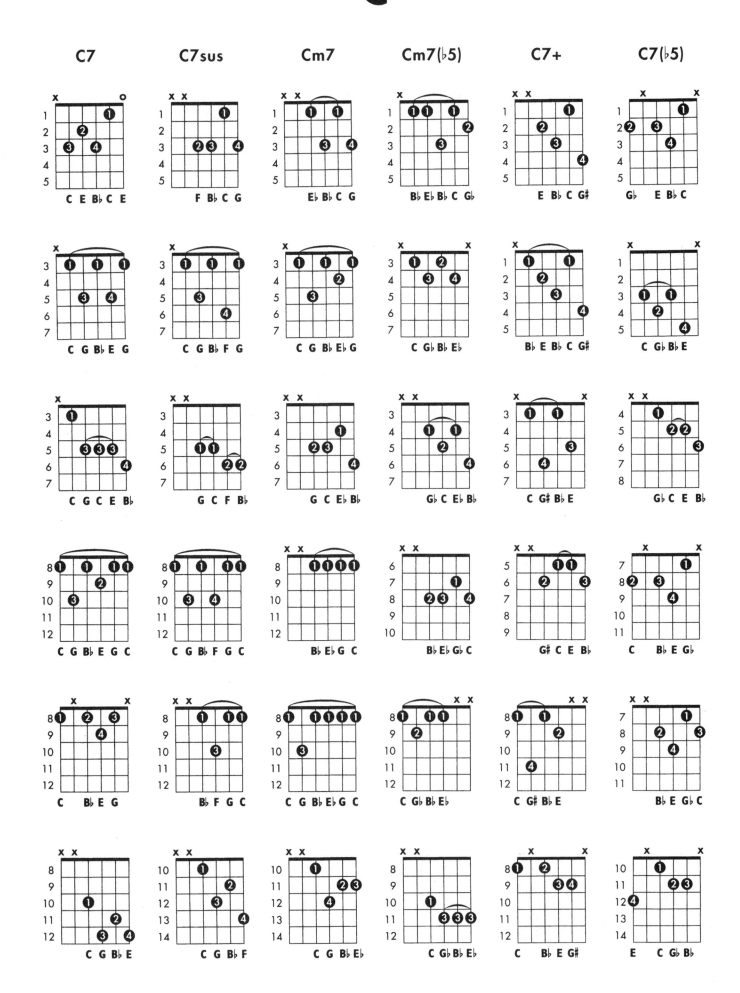

C7   C7sus   Cm7   Cm7(♭5)   C7+   C7(♭5)

C

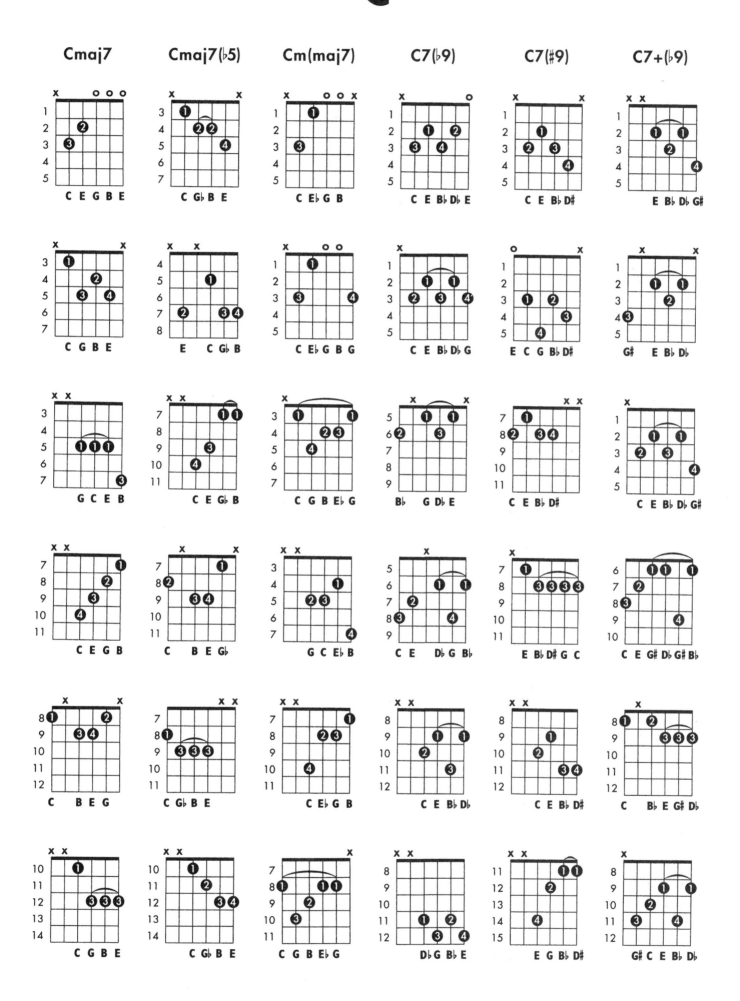

D♭

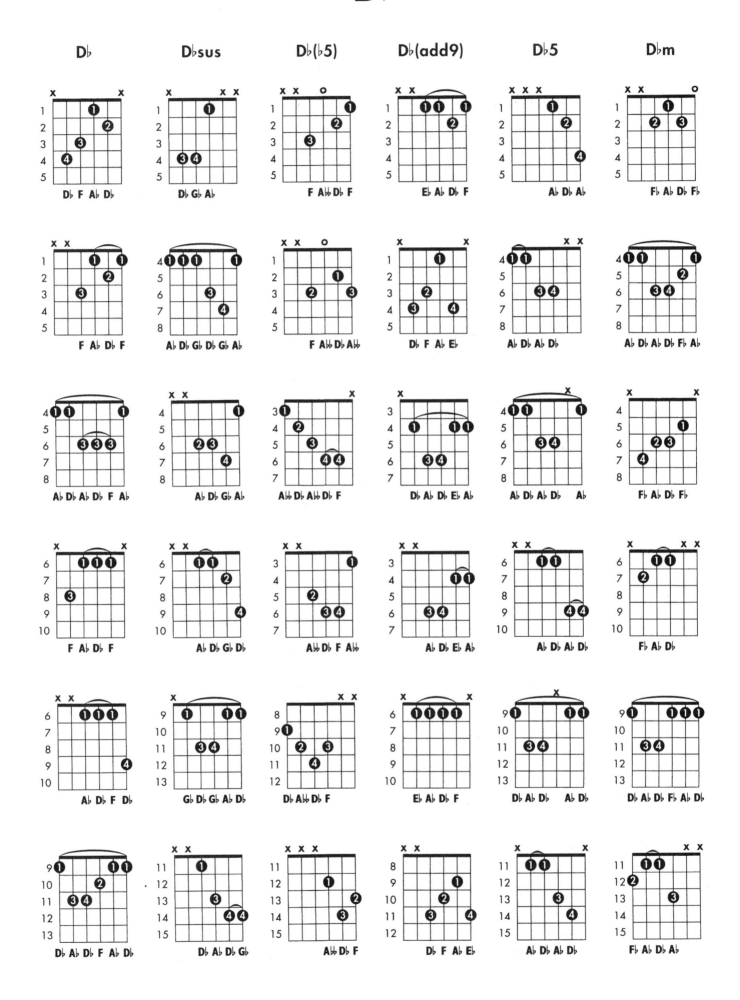

D♭

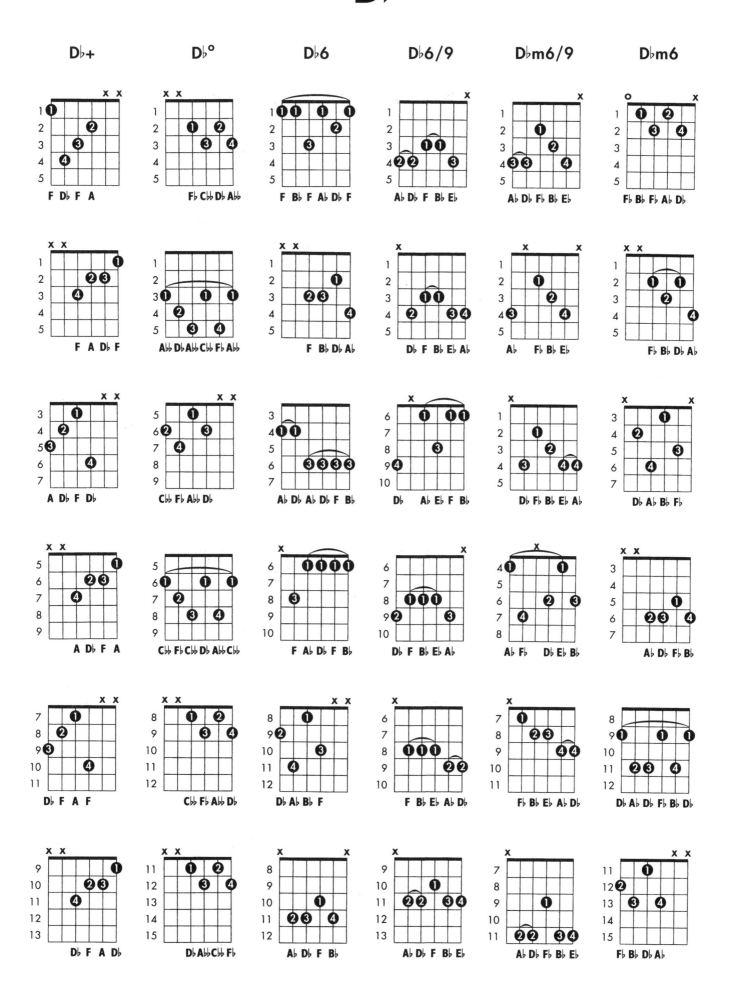

D♭

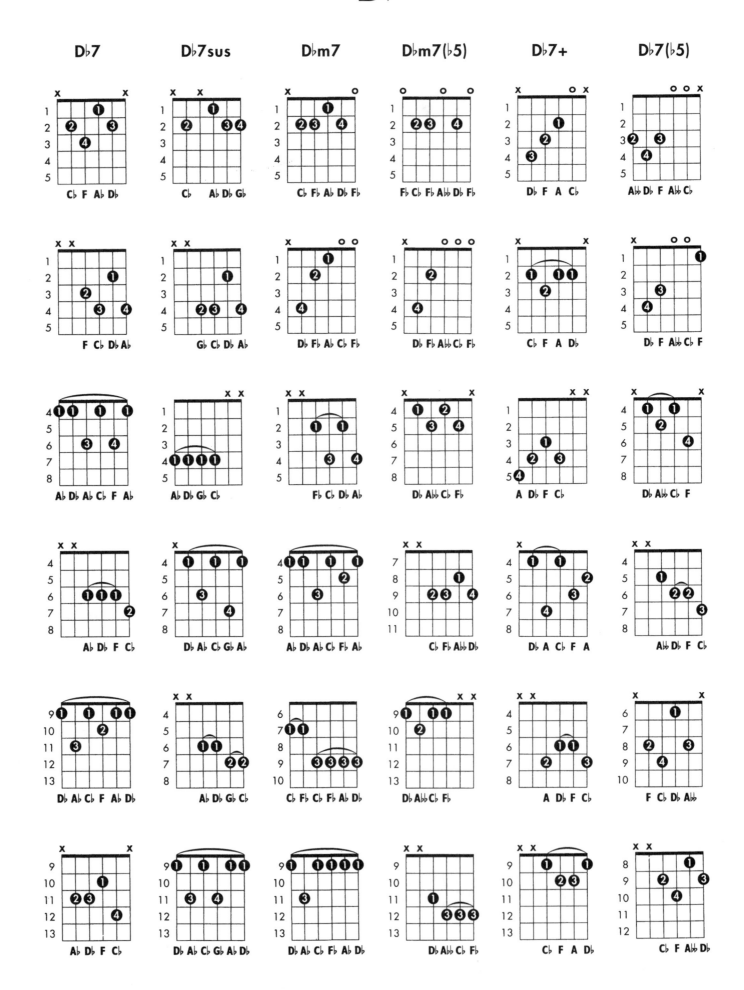

D♭

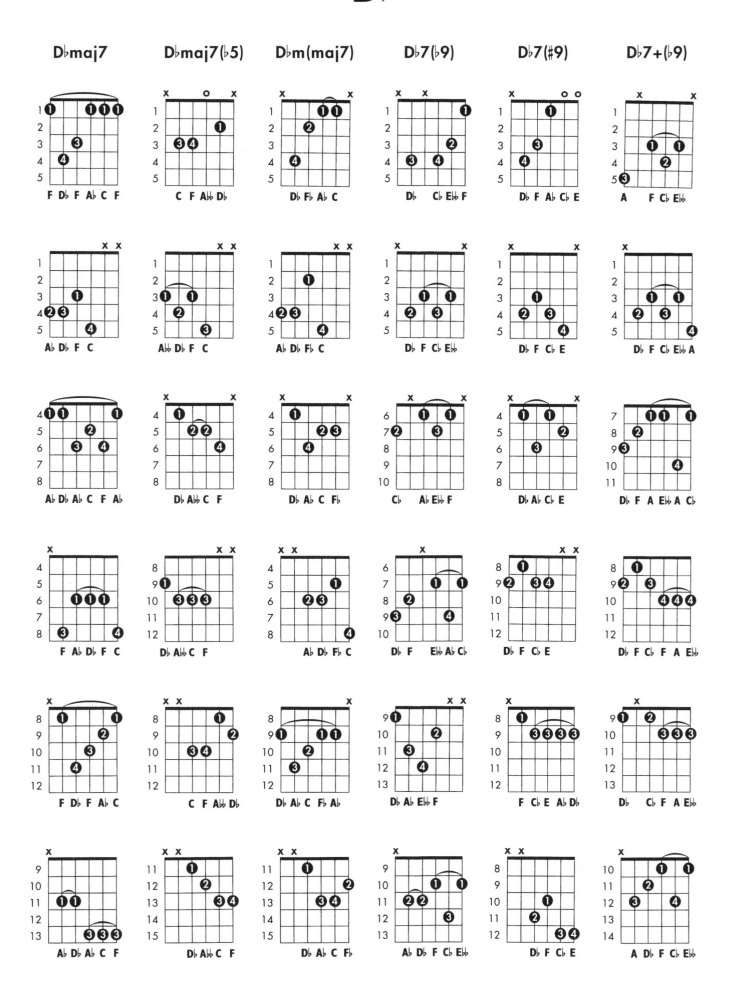

D

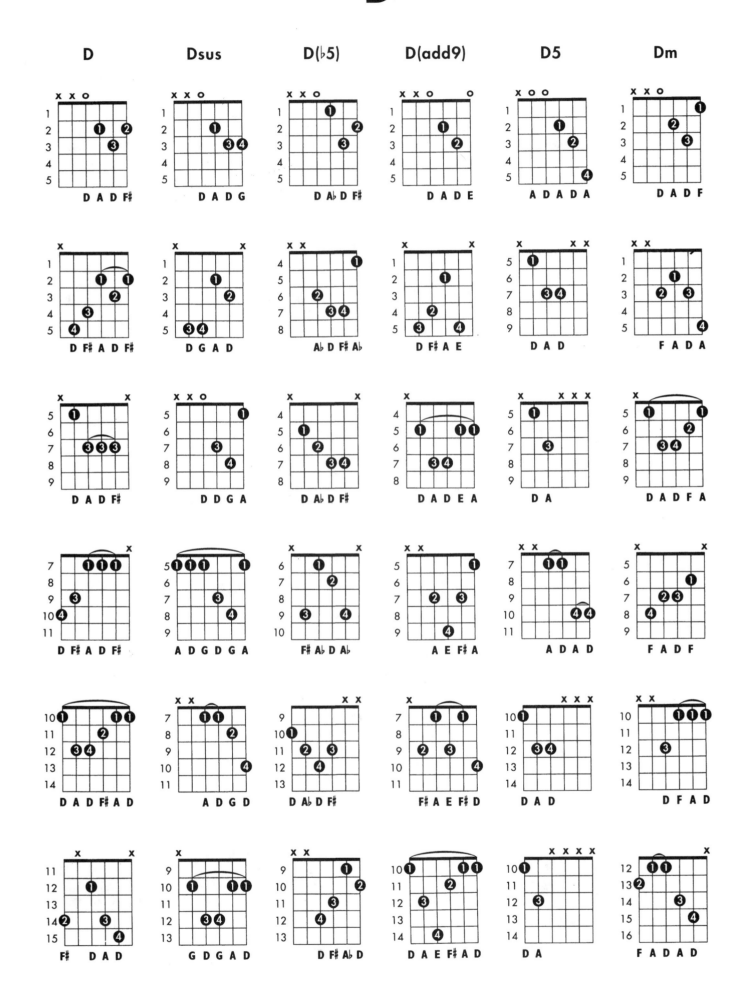

D

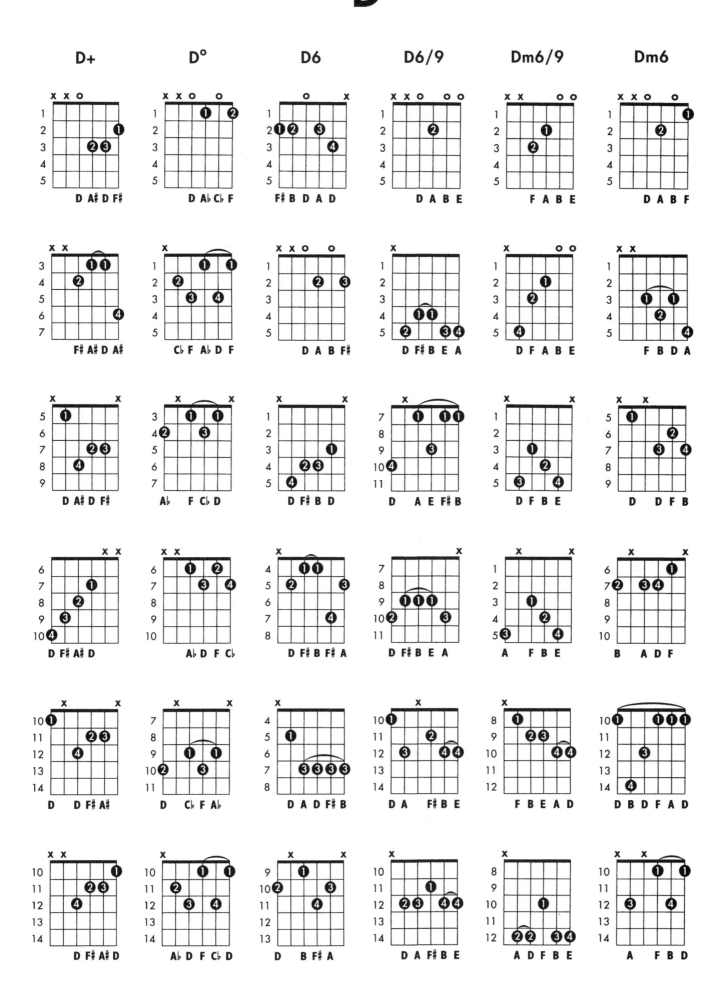

D

| D7 | D7sus | Dm7 | Dm7(♭5) | D7+ | D7(♭5) |

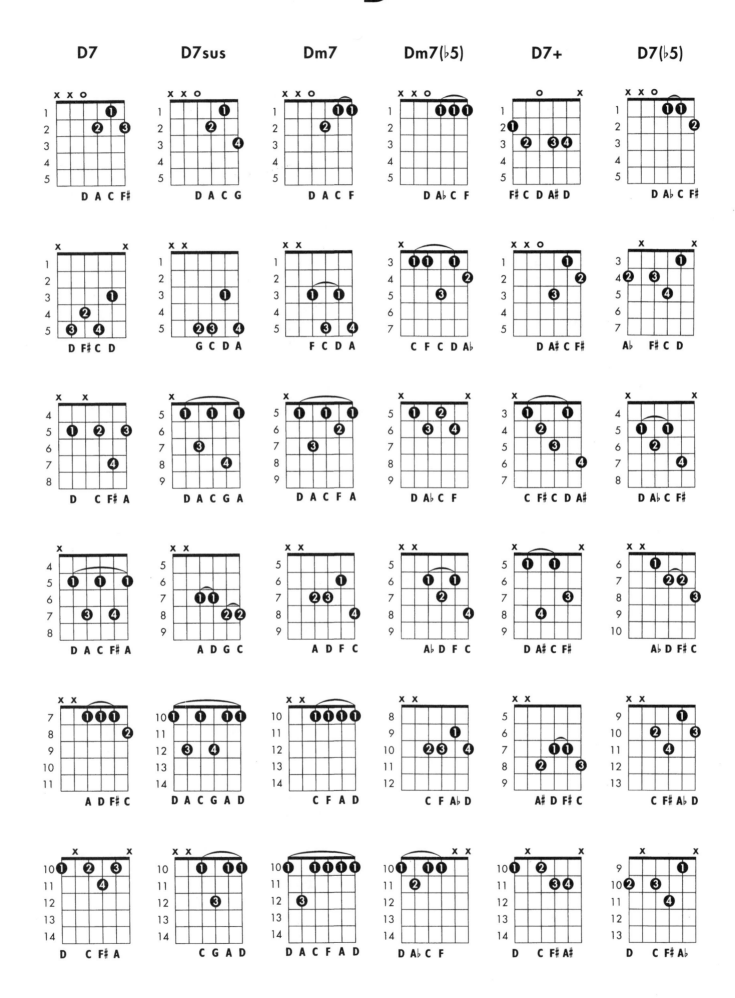

Row 1:
- D7: x x o — D A C F#
- D7sus: x x o — D A C G
- Dm7: x x o — D A C F
- Dm7(♭5): x x o — D A♭ C F
- D7+: o x — F# C D A# D
- D7(♭5): x x o — D A♭ C F#

Row 2:
- D7: x x — D F# C D
- D7sus: x x — G C D A
- Dm7: x x — F C D A
- Dm7(♭5): x — C F C D A♭
- D7+: x x o — D A# C F#
- D7(♭5): x x — A♭ F# C D

Row 3:
- D7: x x — D C F# A
- D7sus: x — D A C G A
- Dm7: x — D A C F A
- Dm7(♭5): x — D A♭ C F
- D7+: x — C F# C D A#
- D7(♭5): x x — D A♭ C F#

Row 4:
- D7: x — D A C F# A
- D7sus: x x — A D G C
- Dm7: x x — A D F C
- Dm7(♭5): x x — A♭ D F C
- D7+: x x — D A# C F#
- D7(♭5): x x — A♭ D F# C

Row 5:
- D7: x x — A D F# C
- D7sus: — D A C G A D
- Dm7: x x — C F A D
- Dm7(♭5): x x — C F A♭ D
- D7+: x x — A# D F# C
- D7(♭5): x x — C F# A♭ D

Row 6:
- D7: x x — D C F# A
- D7sus: x x — C G A D
- Dm7: — D A C F A D
- Dm7(♭5): x x — D A♭ C F
- D7+: x x — D C F# A#
- D7(♭5): x x — D C F# A♭

D

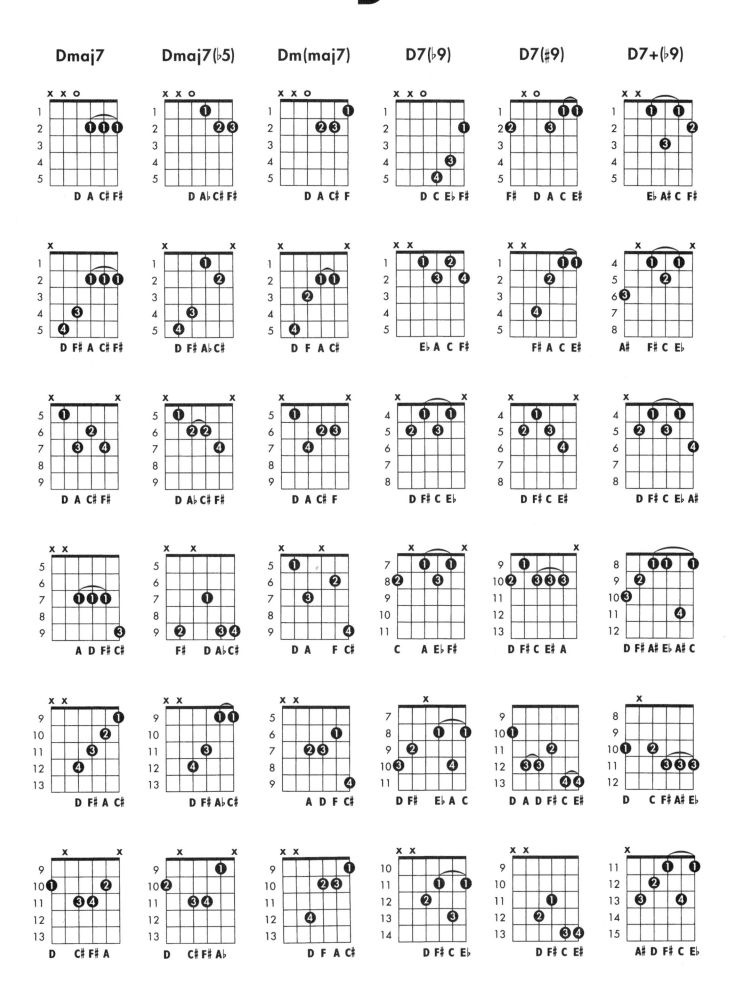

E♭

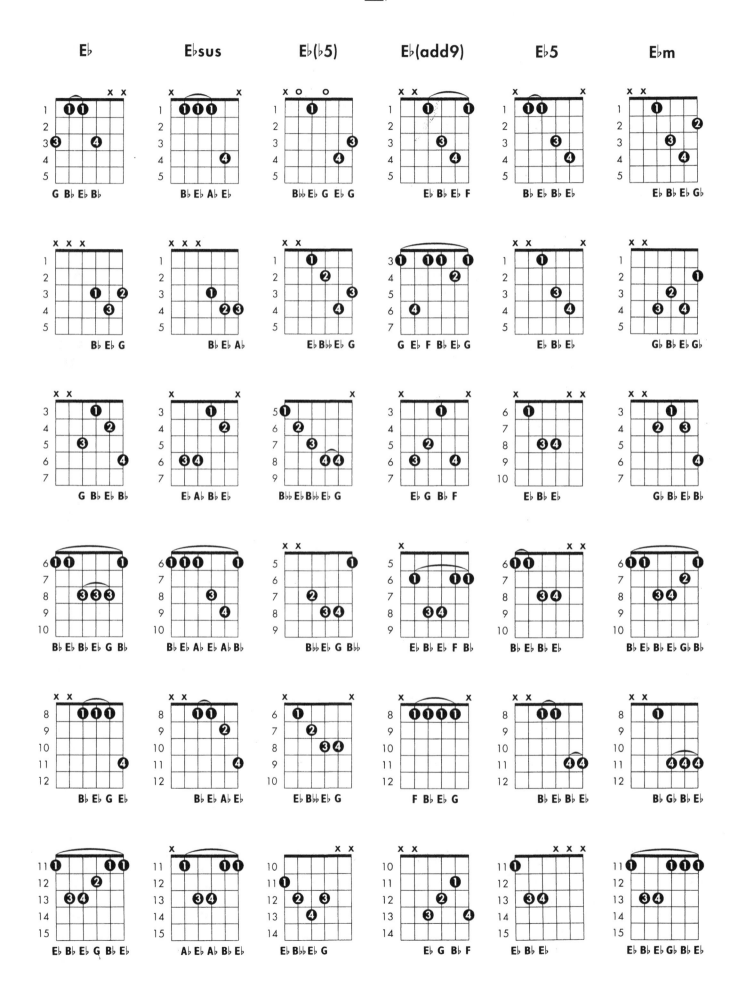

E♭

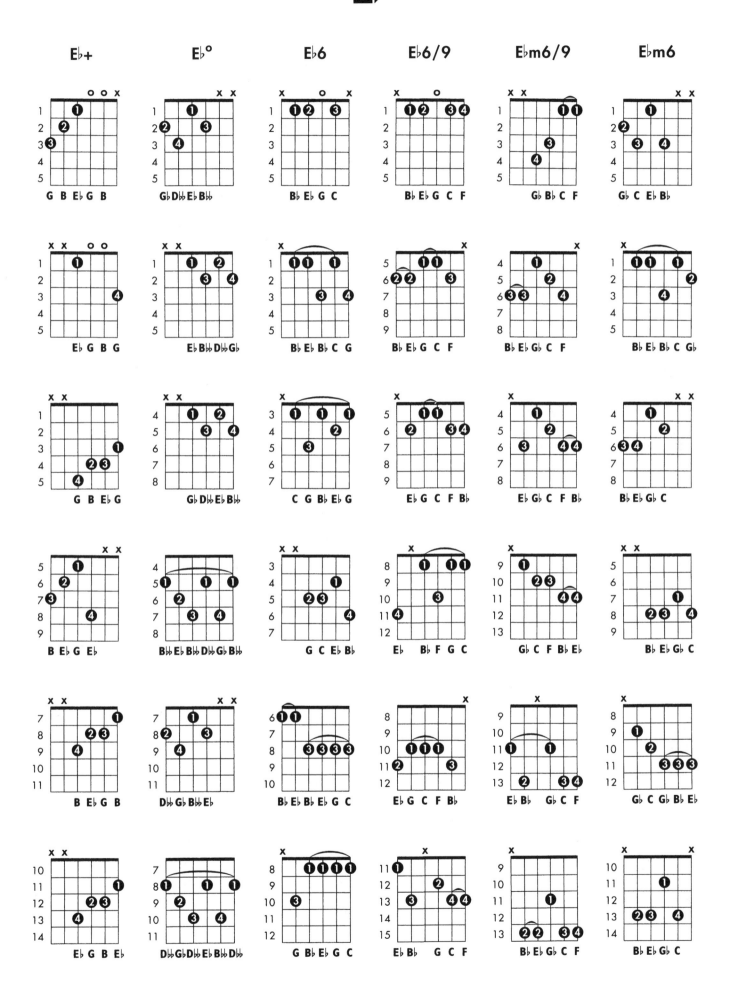

E♭

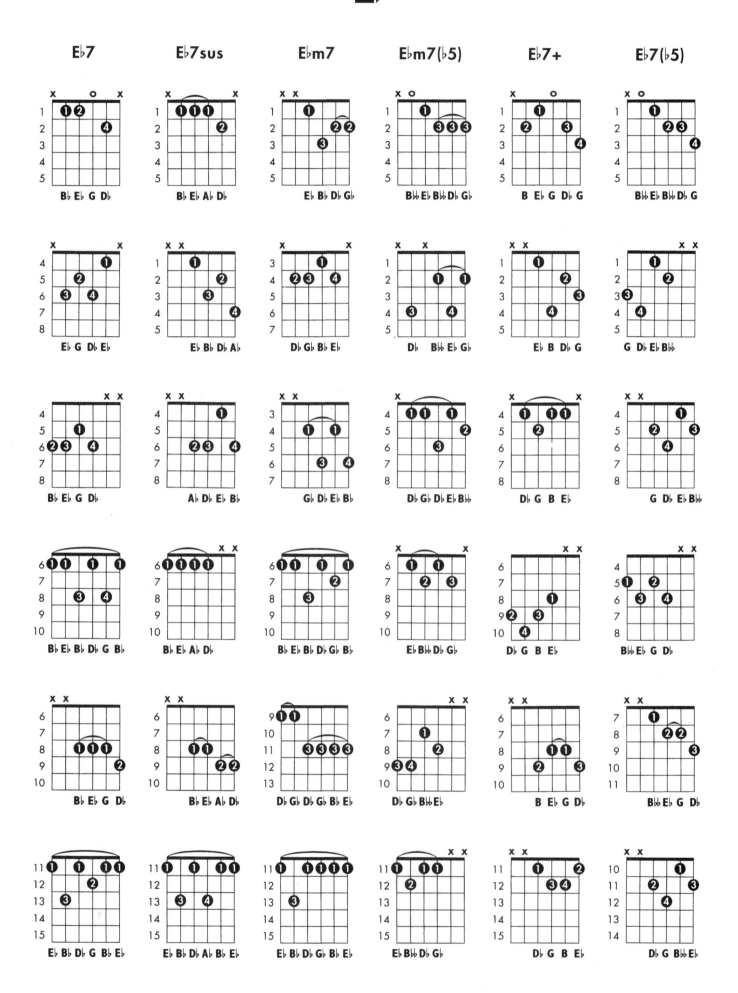

E♭

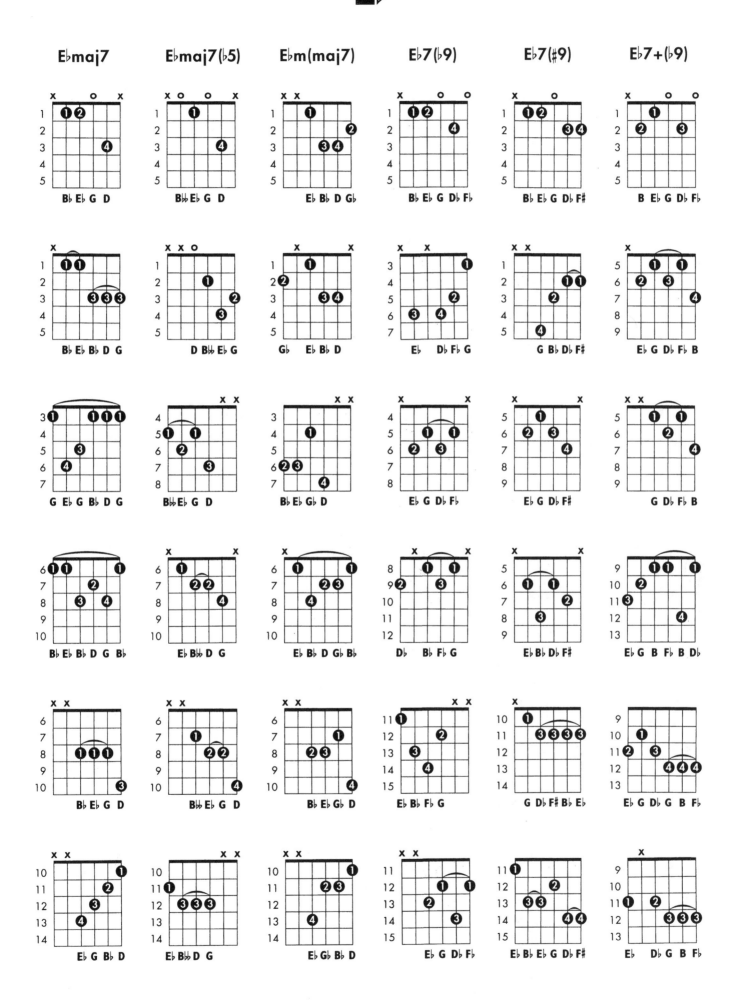

E

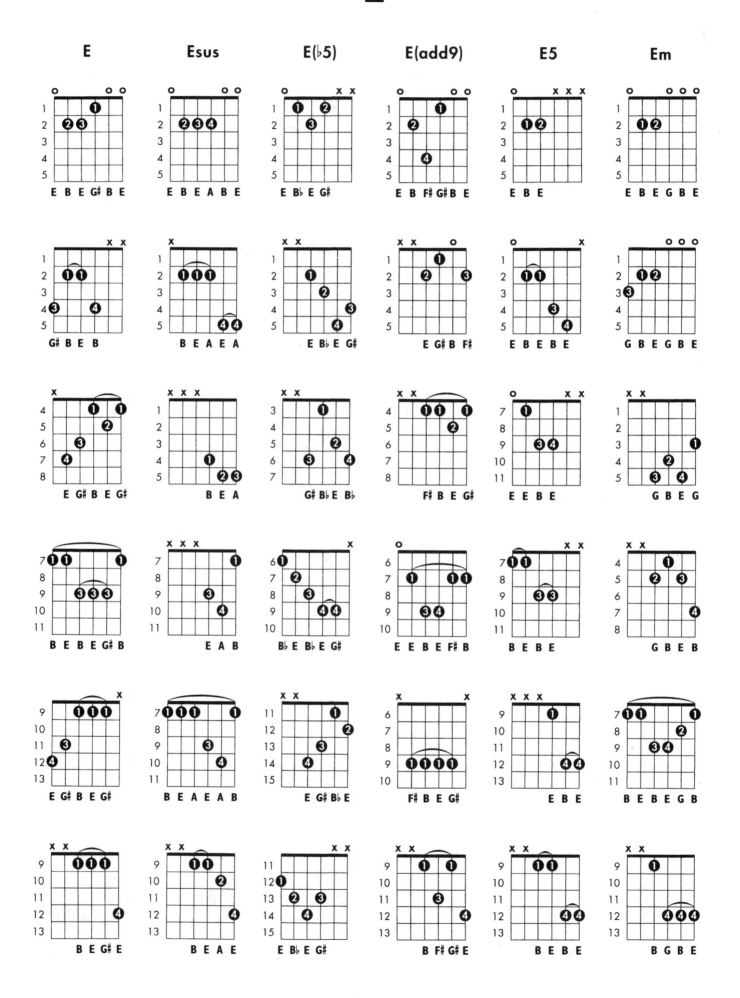

E

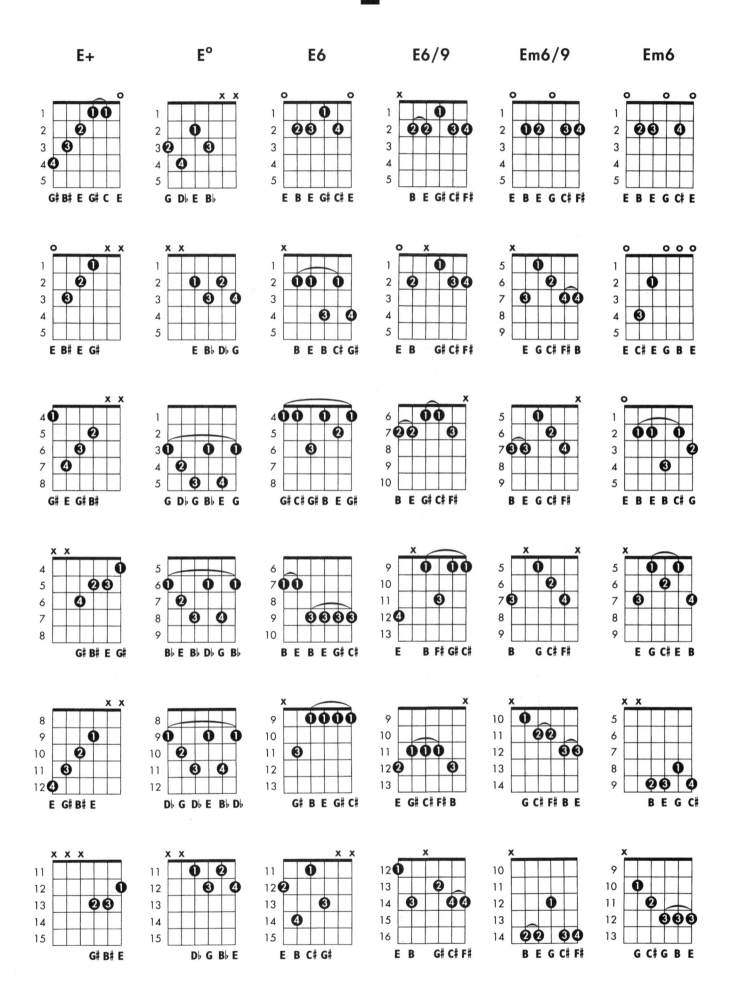

E

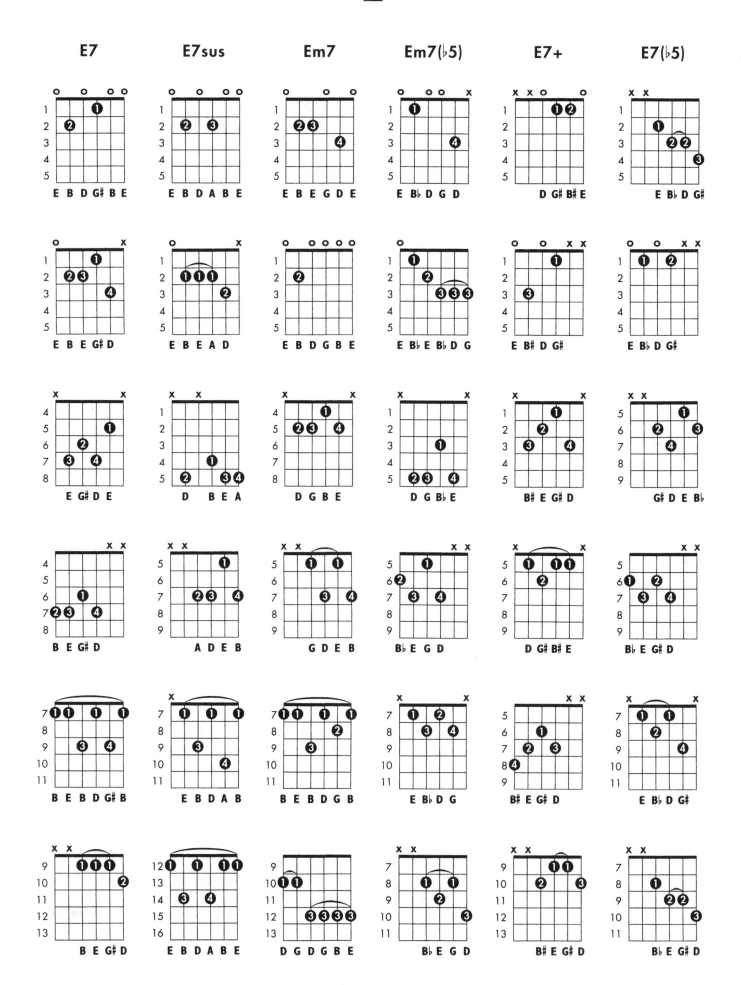

E

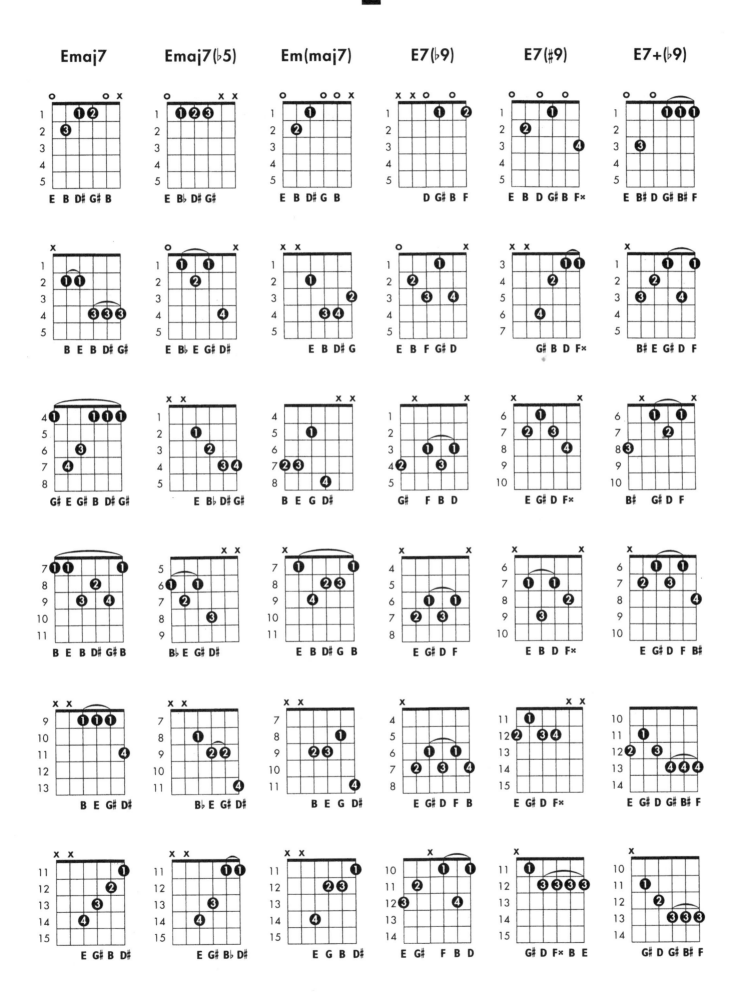

F

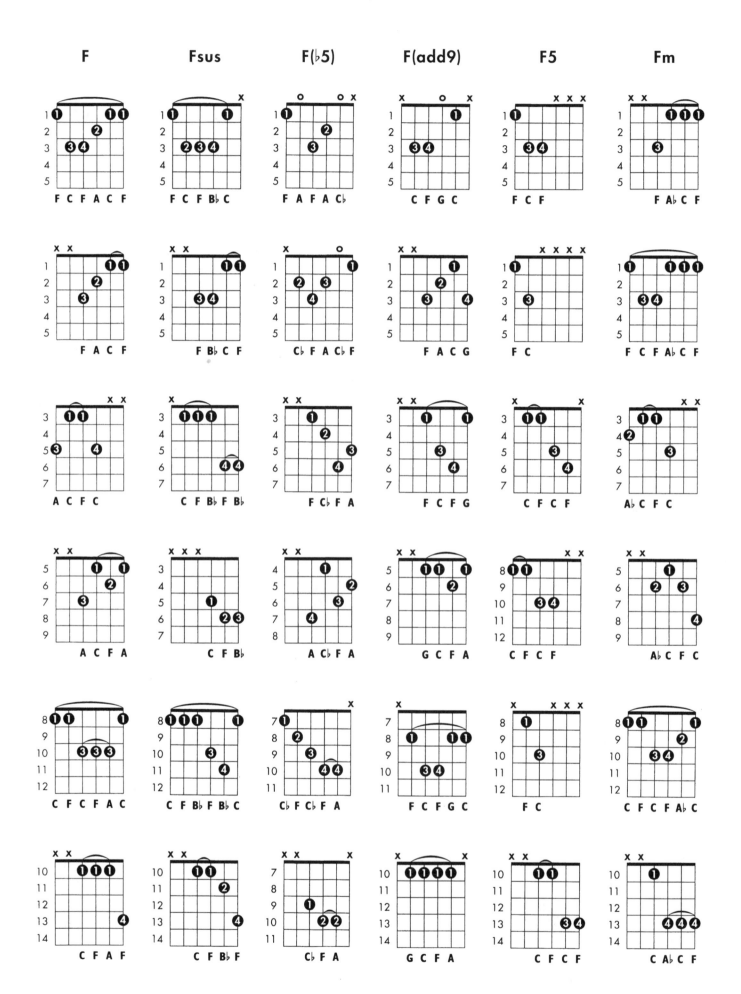

F

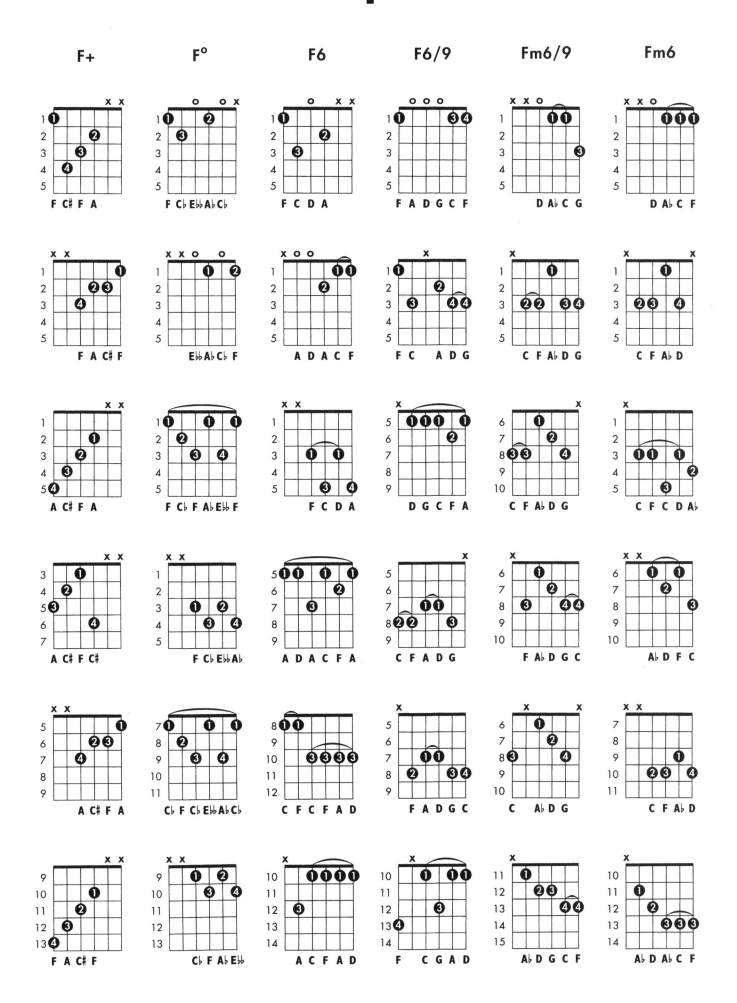

F

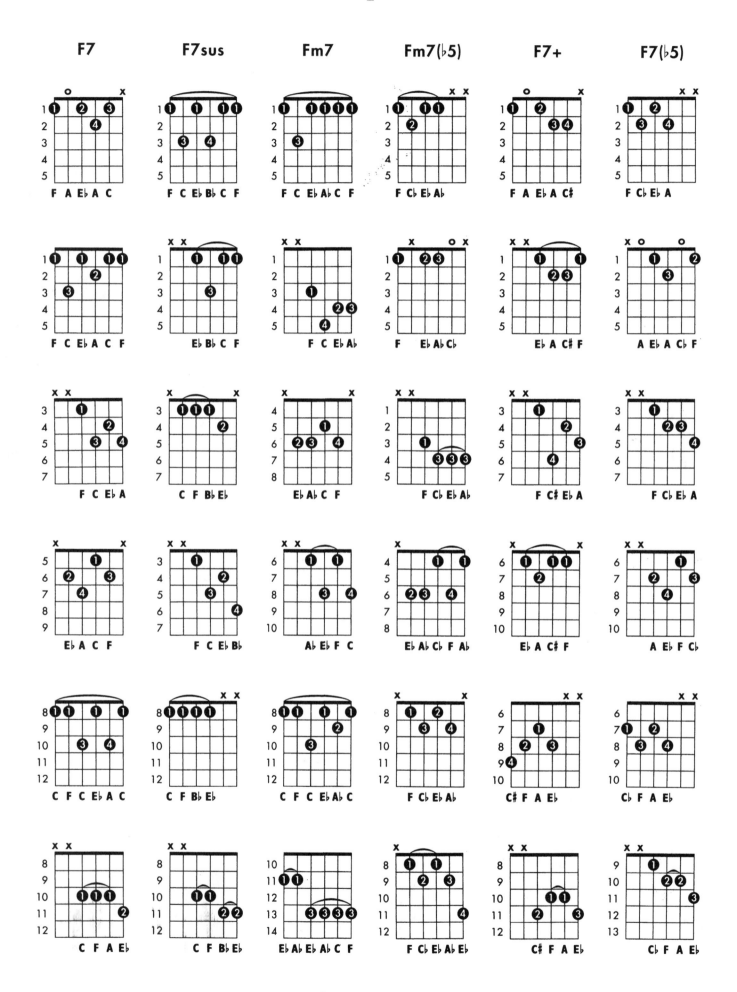

F

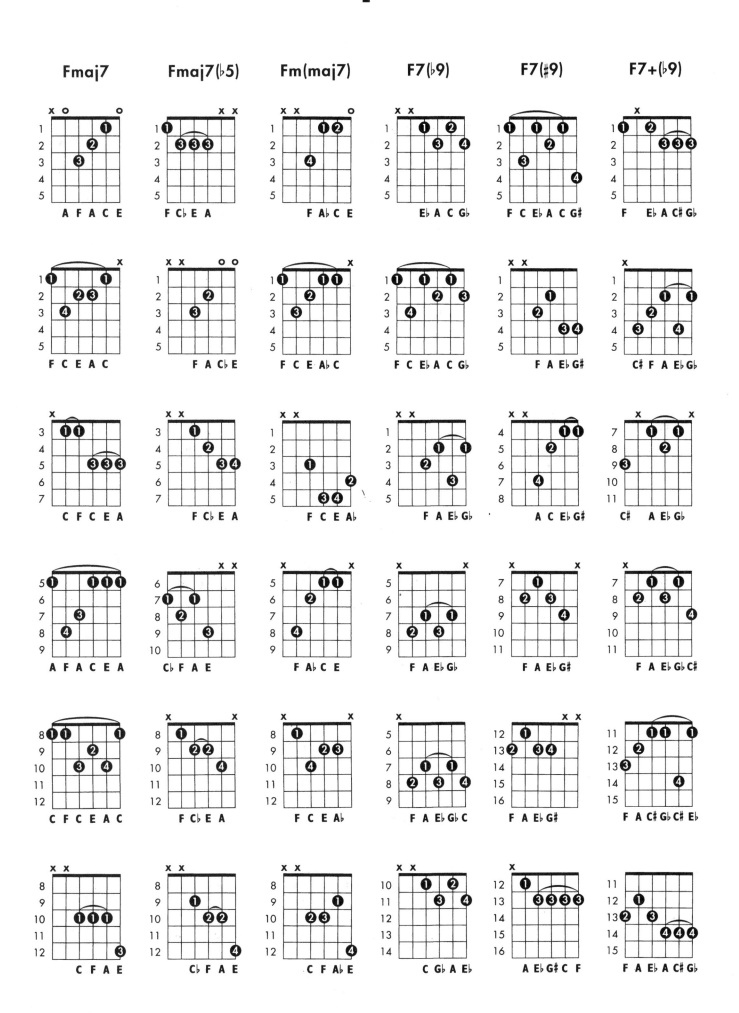

F#

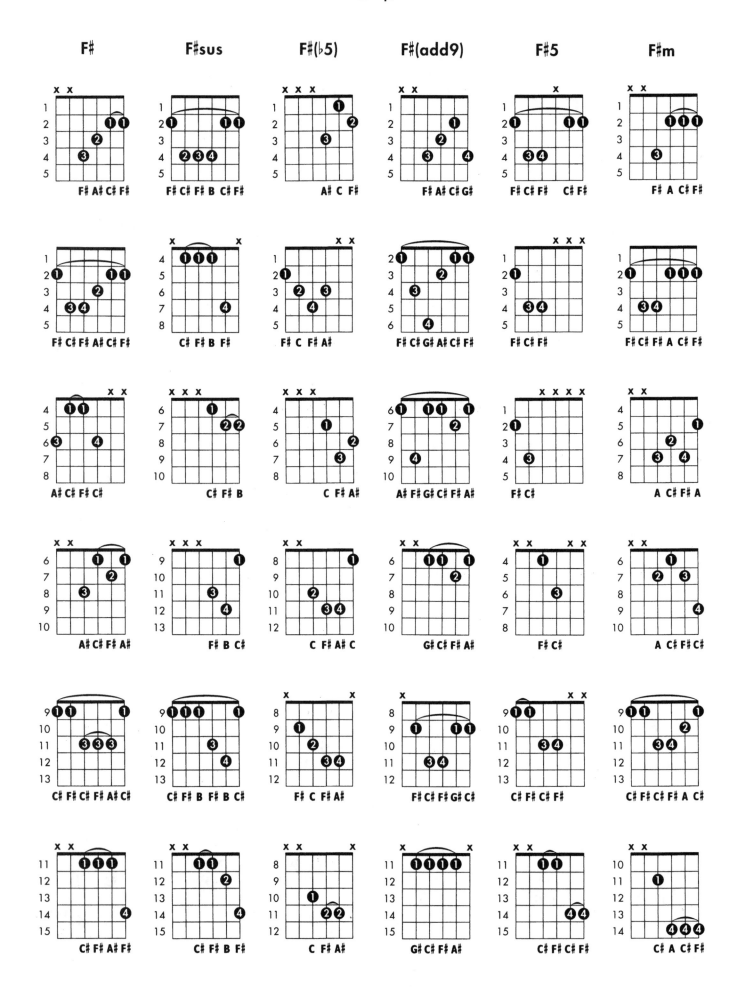

F#

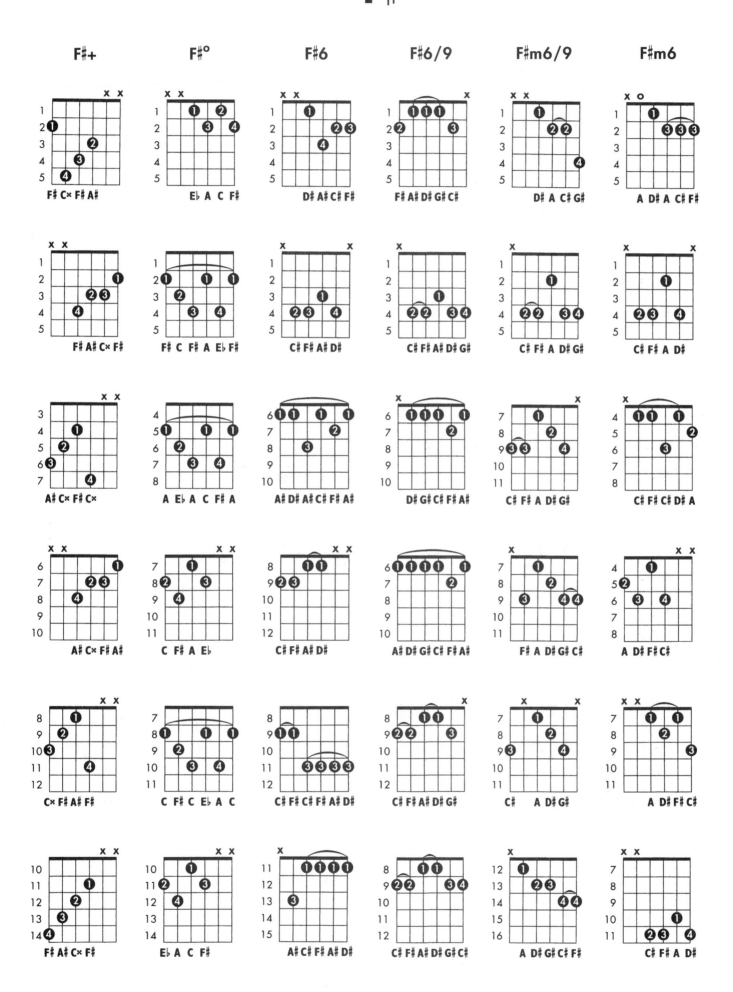

F#

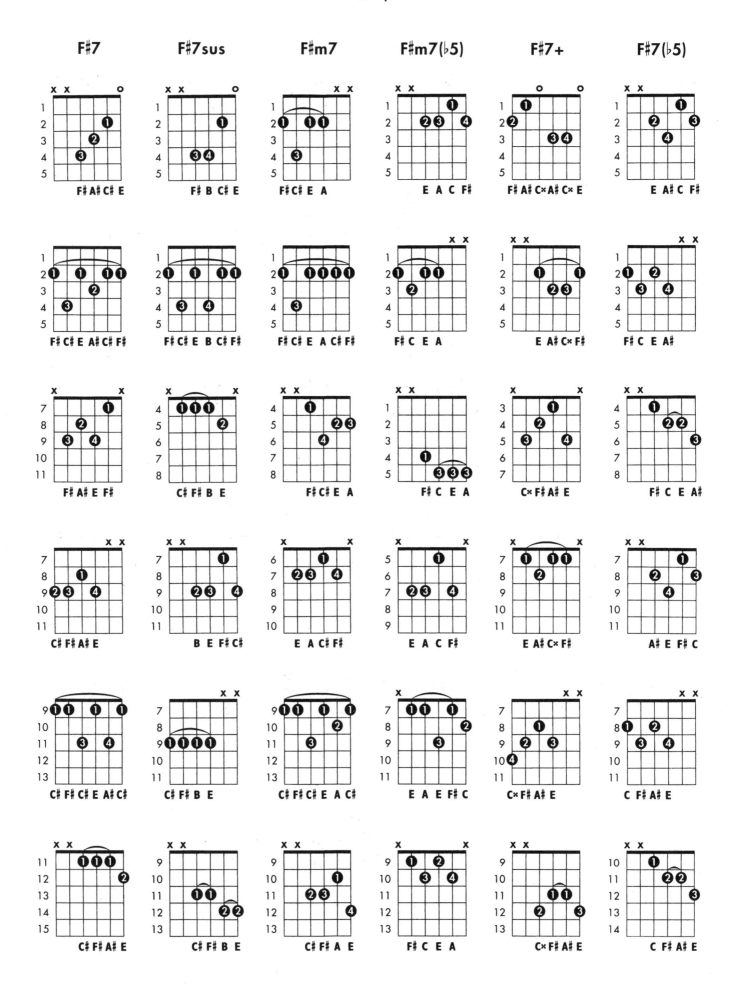

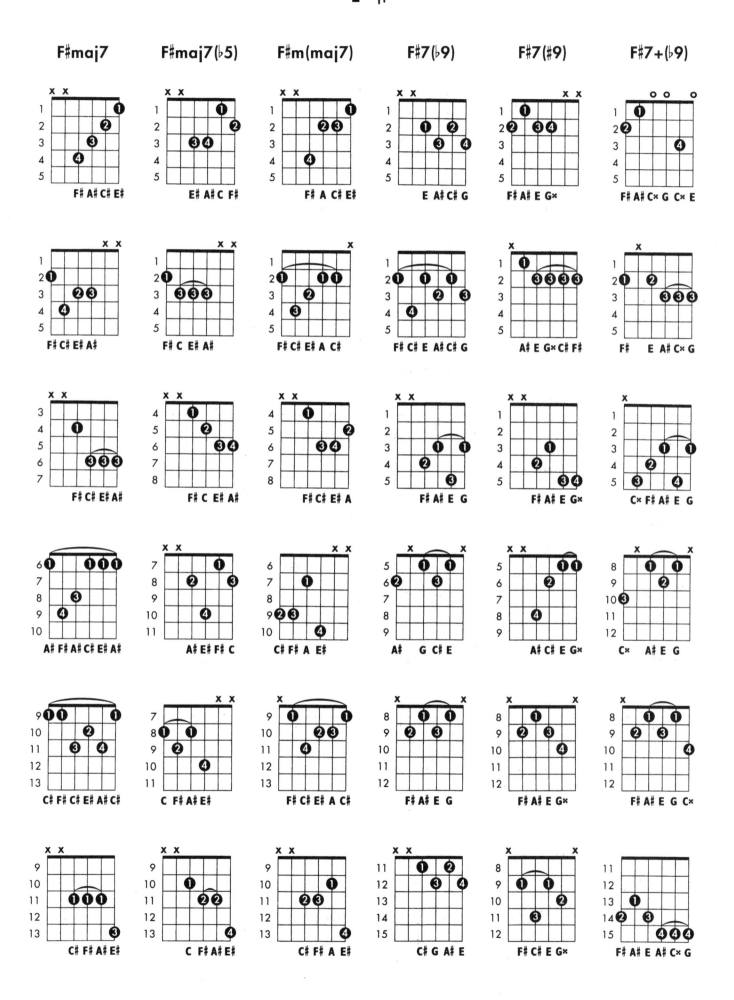

F#

G

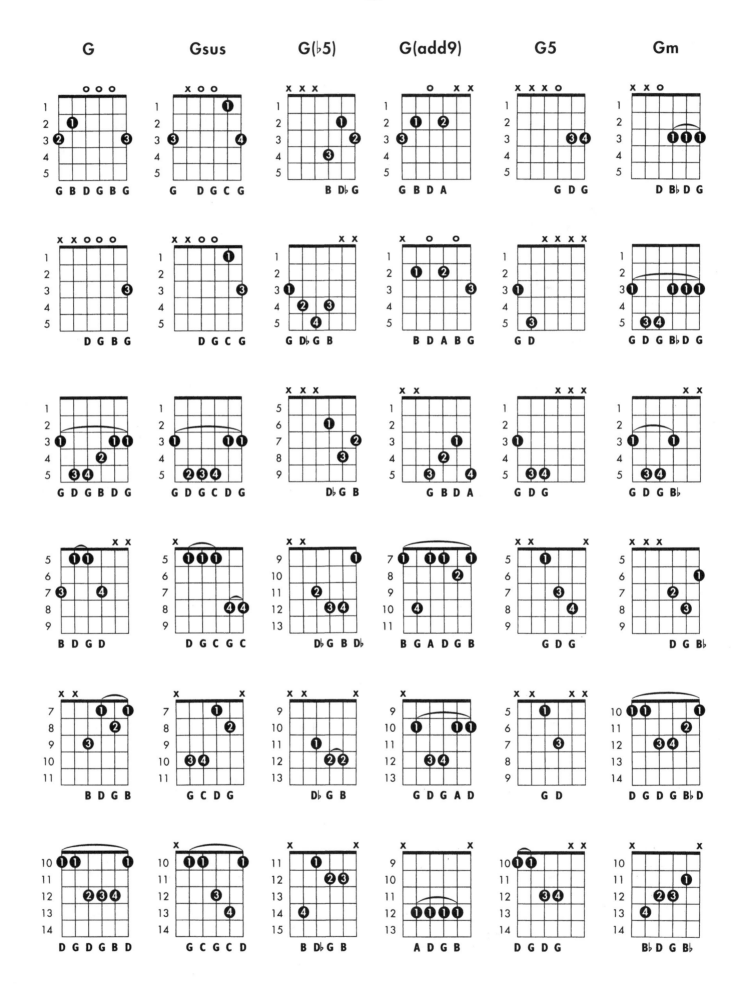

G

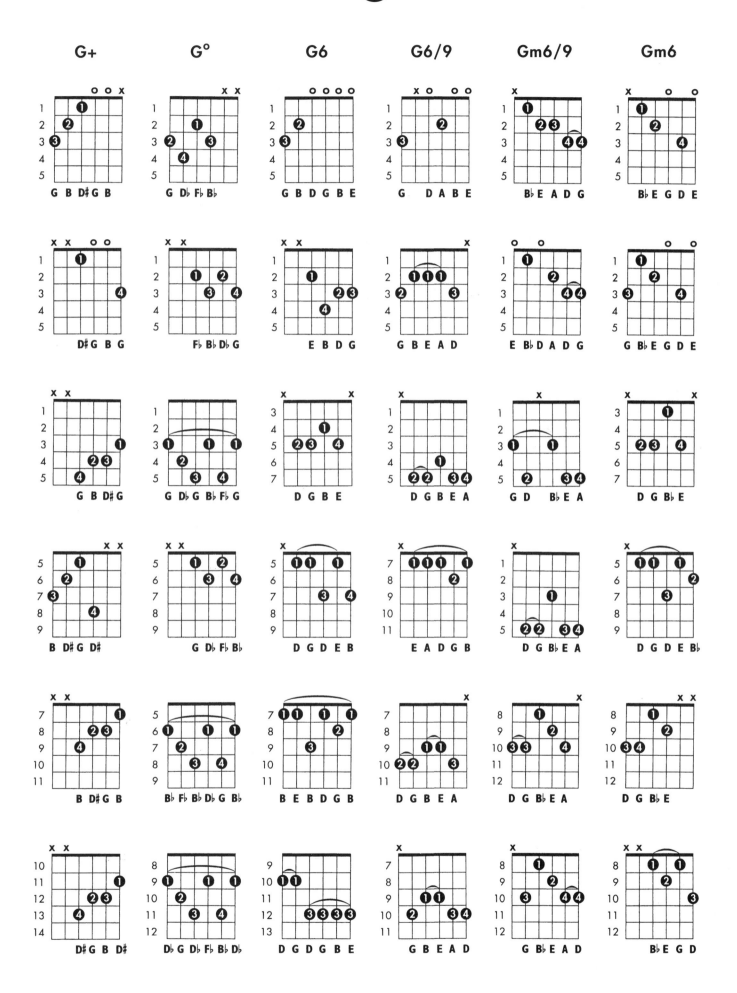

G

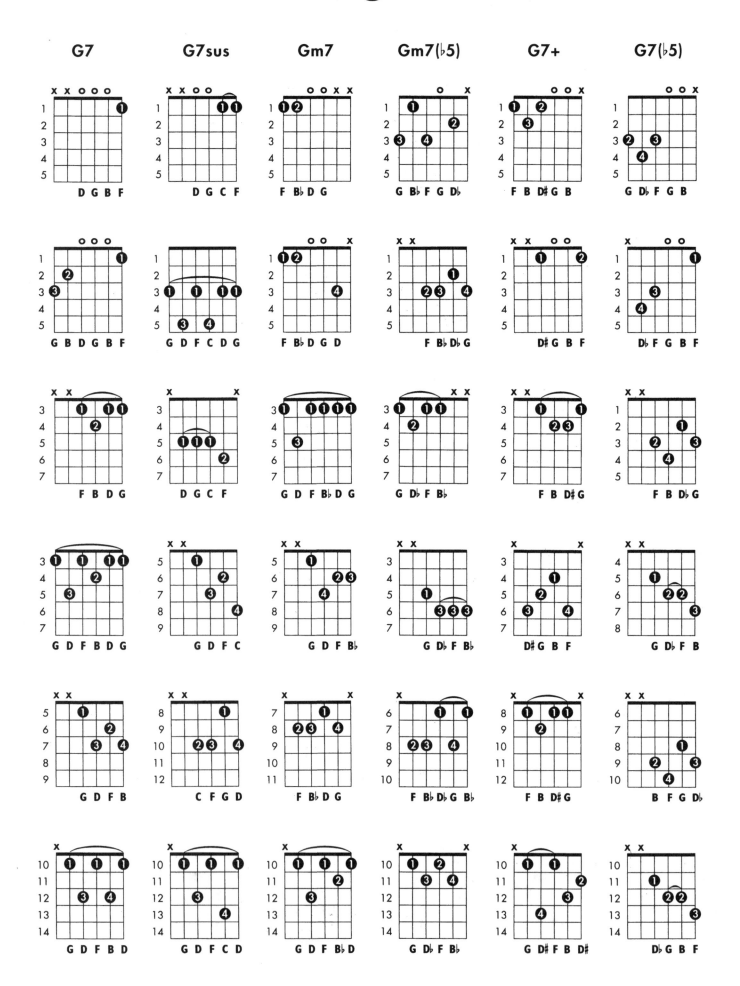

G

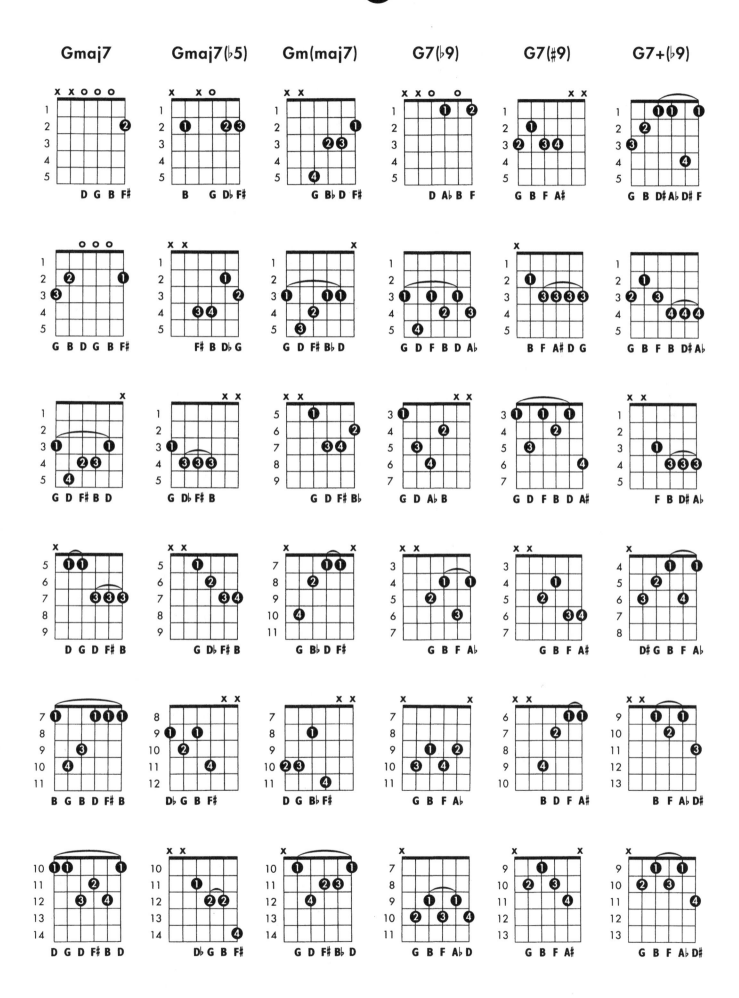

A♭

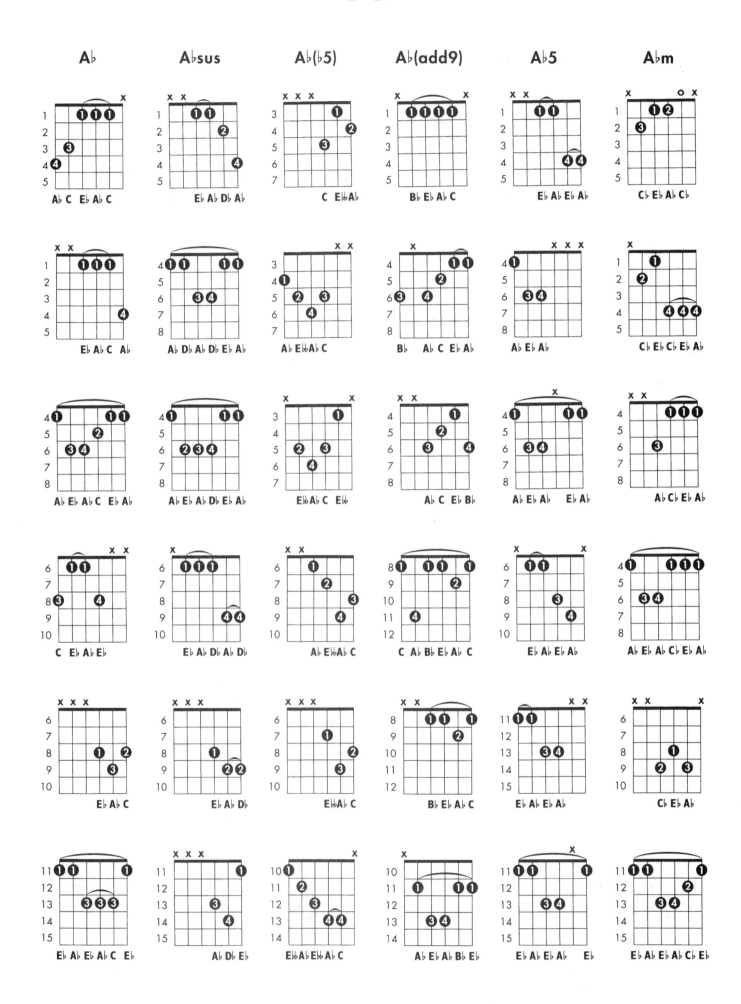

A♭

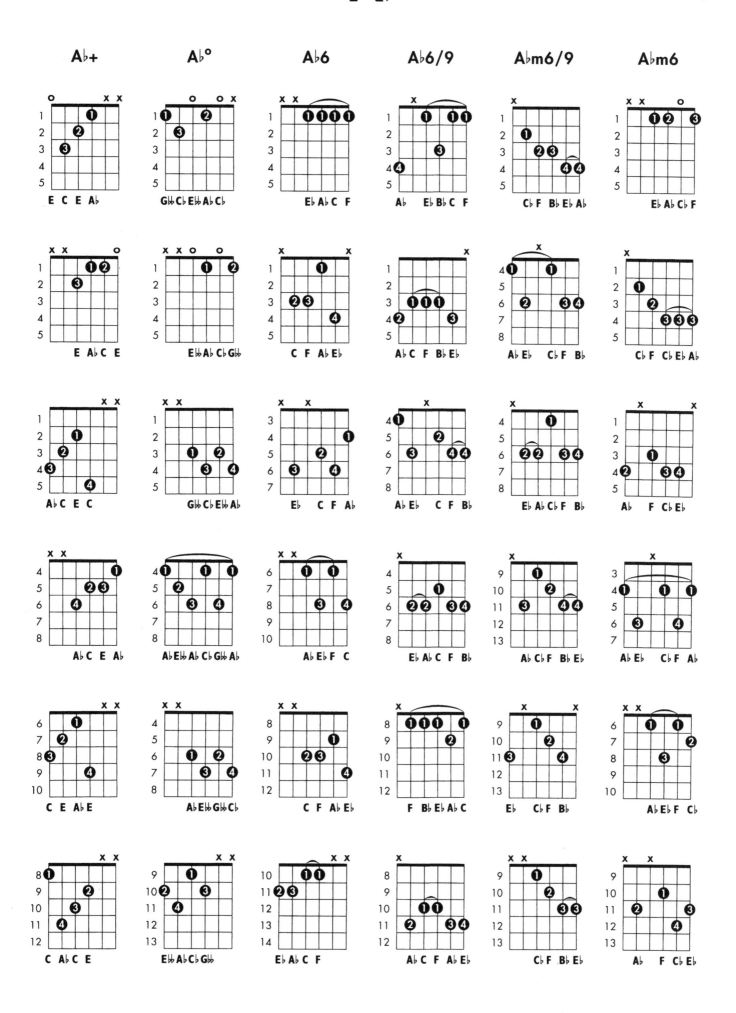

A♭

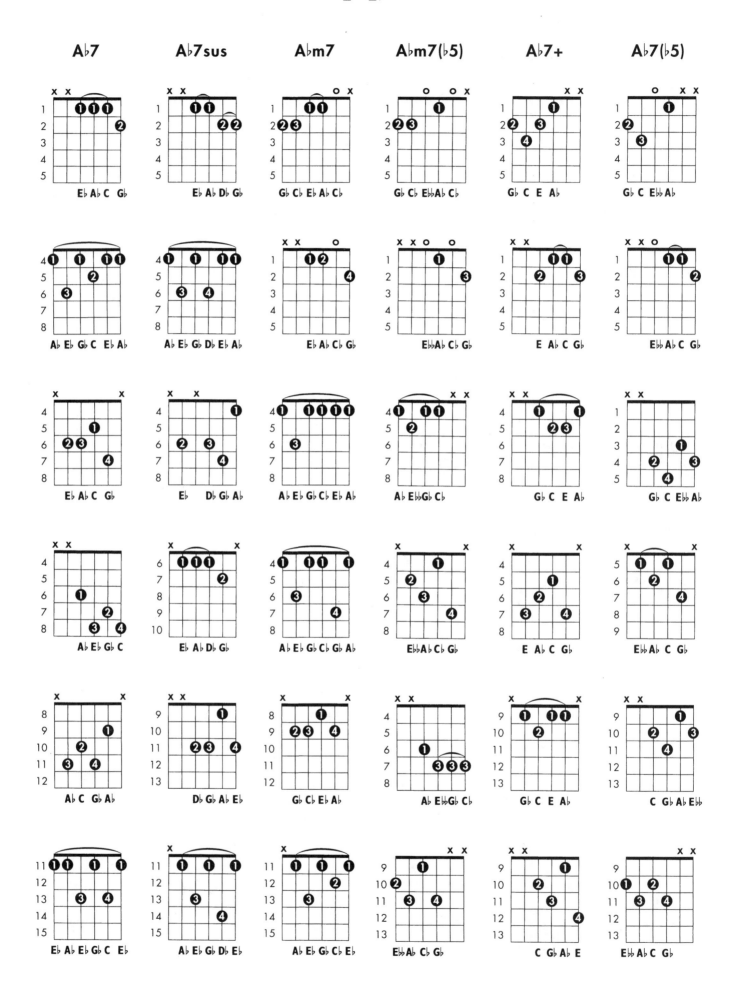

A♭

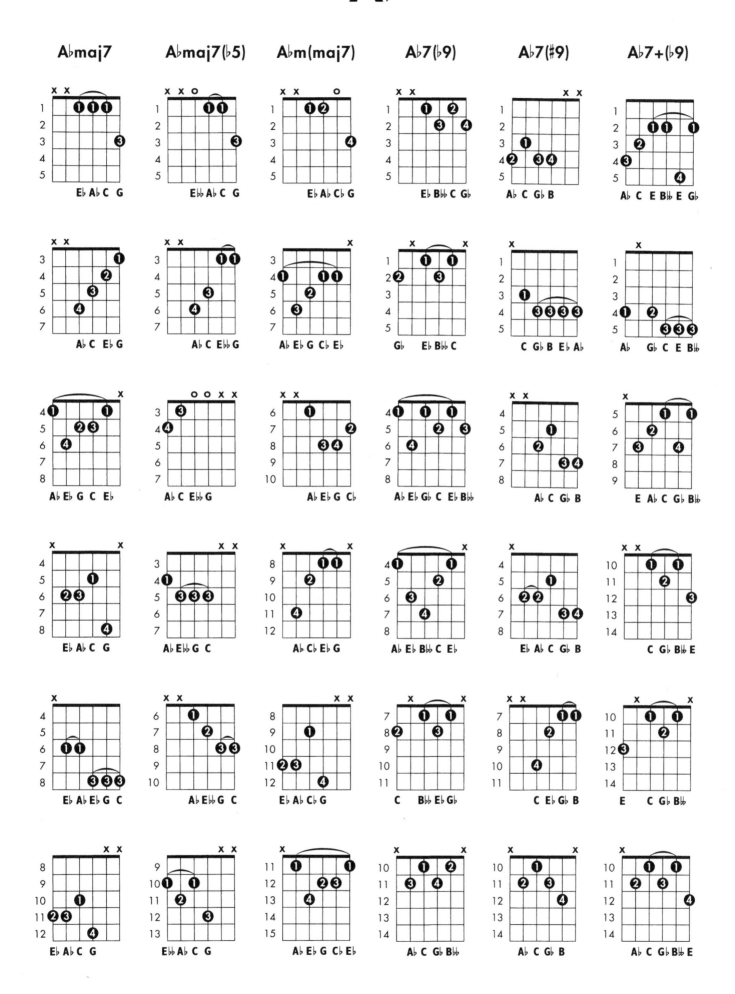

Guitar Fingerboard Chart
Frets 1–12

STRINGS

6th 5th 4th 3rd 2nd 1st
E A D G B E

Fret	6th	5th	4th	3rd	2nd	1st
Open	E	A	D	G	B	E
1st Fret	F	A#/B♭	D#/E♭	G#/A♭	C	F
2nd Fret	F#/G♭	B	E	A	C#/D♭	F#/G♭
3rd Fret	G	C	F	A#/B♭	D	G
4th Fret	G#/A♭	C#/D♭	F#/G♭	B	D#/E♭	G#/A♭
5th Fret	A	D	G	C	E	A
6th Fret	A#/B♭	D#/E♭	G#/A♭	C#/D♭	F	A#/B♭
7th Fret	B	E	A	D	F#/G♭	B
8th Fret	C	F	A#/B♭	D#/E♭	G	C
9th Fret	C#/D♭	F#/G♭	B	E	G#/A♭	C#/D♭
10th Fret	D	G	C	F	A	D
11th Fret	D#/E♭	G#/A♭	C#/D♭	F#/G♭	A#/B♭	D#/E♭
12th Fret	E	A	D	G	B	E

STRINGS

Fingerboard note names (fret by fret):

- 1st Fret: F, B♭, E♭, A♭, C, F (also A#, D#, G#)
- 2nd Fret: F#/G♭, B, E, A, D♭/G♭ (also C#, F#)
- 3rd Fret: G, C, F, B♭, D, G (also A#)
- 4th Fret: A♭/D♭/G♭, B, E♭, A♭ (also G#, C#, F#, D#, G#)
- 5th Fret: A, D, G, C, E, A
- 6th Fret: B♭, E♭, A♭, D♭, F, B♭ (also A#, D#, G#, C#, A#)
- 7th Fret: B, E, A, D, G♭, B (also F#)
- 8th Fret: C, F, B♭, E♭, G, C (also A#, D#)
- 9th Fret: D♭, G♭, B, E, A♭, D♭ (also C#, F#, G#, C#)
- 10th Fret: D, G, C, F, A, D
- 11th Fret: E♭, A♭, D♭, G♭, B♭, E♭ (also D#, G#, C#, F#, A#, D#)
- 12th Fret: E, A, D, G, B, E